ELEGANT EATING

ELEGANT EATING

Four hundred years of dining in style

❖

EDITED BY PHILIPPA GLANVILLE
AND HILARY YOUNG

V&A Publications

First published by V&A Publications, 2002

© 2002 The Board of Trustees of the
Victoria and Albert Museum

The contributors assert their moral rights to be identified
as the authors of this book.

ISBN 1 85177 337 1

A catalogue record of this book is available from the
British Library.

All rights reserved. No part of this publication may be
reproduced, stored in a retrieval system, or transmitted in any
form or by any means, electronic, mechanical, photocopying,
recording or otherwise, without the prior written permission of
the Publishers.

New V&A photographs by Richard Davis
Designed by Bernard Higton
Project management by Geoff Barlow

Printed in Hong Kong

Jacket illustration: Assemblage of English tablewares; see page
136 for details.

Endpaper illustration: Dessert table, engraving, from François
Massialot, *Nouvelle instruction pour les confitures, les liqueurs,
et les fruits*, Paris, revised edition, 1740 (NAL)

Weights of silver appearing in this book are given in
Troy ounces (1 Troy ounce = 31.1 grams).

SOUTHAMPTON INSTITUTE
LIBRARY SERVICES LTD
SUPPLIER DAWSON3
ORDER No S/0
DATE 27·3·02

V&A Publications
160 Brompton Road
London SW3 1HW
www.vam.ac.uk

CONTENTS

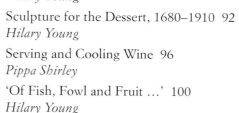

ACKNOWLEDGEMENTS

We are indebted to Bill Brown; N. & I. Franklin; Simon Jervis; Charles Truman of C. & L. Burman, Works of Art, and to a number of private collectors for lending items for photography. For generously supplying photographs, or waiving reproduction fees, we would like to thank the following: the Association of British Designer Silversmiths; Brian Beet; The Bluebird Restaurant, London; Karin Walton at Bristol City Museum and Art Gallery; China House, London; Richard Dennis Publications; Christopher Fry; Rita Gans; Thomas Goode; The Hempel, London; Hoogsteder and Hoogsteder, The Hague; The Incorporation of Goldsmiths of the City of Edinburgh; The Warden and Fellows of New College, Oxford; Oxford University Press; The Ritz, London; Ole Willumsen Krog at the Royal Palace, Copenhagen; The Savoy Hotel, Helsinki; Sheffield City Council; Christopher English at the Silver Trust; Peter Ting; the staff of Waddesdon Manor, Buckinghamshire; the Duke of Wellington; The Librarian, David Beasley, and the Court of the Worshipful Company of Goldsmiths, London.

For assistance or advice, our thanks go also to Mary Balkwill, Robin Emmerson, Patricia Ferguson, Jonathan Marsden, Laurence Mauderli, David Mitchell, Lord Rothschild, Selma Schwartz, Sam Segal, Ruth Smith, Timothy Stevens, the Hon. Georgina Stonor, the Duke of Wellington and Christopher Woolgar.

All new V&A photographs for the book were taken by Richard Davis of the museum's photographic studio, to whom we are enormously indebted – not only for his excellent photographs, but also for his patience and good humour. We would also like to thank our colleagues Terry Bloxham, Clare Browne, Louise Hofman, Ken Jackson, Valerie Mendes, Rebecca Naylor and Steve Woodhouse. Finally, we owe an enormous debt of gratitude to Mary Butler and her hard-working team at V&A Publications; to Geoff Barlow, our project manager; to Slaney Begley, our copy editor; and to Bernard Higton, our excellent designer; all of whose efforts have done so much to ensure the success of the book.

ℐNTRODUCTION

There is something special about a formal dinner. Trouble is taken, people dress up – servants in livery or 'waiters' black and white' and guests in clean clothes and jewels – there are rituals, a setting is lit and decorated, lavish attention is given to the details of serving and eating, and food and drink are generously offered. This sense of theatre, of the acting out of a dramatic performance in which all play their part, is about taste or *goût* as much as consumption. A dinner is sadly evanescent; once over, it may be recalled through a painting, a photograph (less often), a memoir or a menu, but its essence lies in the associated memories of good company, ambience and good cheer – a special occasion.

This book explores the material culture of eating, a universal experience that differs subtly between social groups, between town and country, between everyday and celebration. It delves into practices that become more obscure as they are described and questions the origins of familiar objects. Take the tureen, invented in the 1690s. When Patrick Lamb, Master-Cook to the royal family published his collection of 'the choicest receipts', *Royal Cookery*, in London in 1710, he found it necessary to define 'A Terreyne Dish, at Court ... made of silver, round and upright, holding about six quarts English measure ... with the handles such as a small cistern has'. The chef was warned to wipe the outside before sending it to table, a reminder that hot soups and stews in special covered vessels were recent arrivals from the French court. New objects often caused problems of terminology, especially in the late seventeenth century when European eating and drinking went through a revolution: in 1659 Elizabeth Murray's London goldsmith struggled to name 'a thing for Shugar' that she had brought from Paris; and the spellings of mazarine, surtout and

Above: Household officers sharing a dinner, each wearing a badge of office. Upper servants followed the dining rituals of their masters.

Left: The menu, like a theatre programme, sets out the order of the event. The word is French, like so many of the elements of dinner.

7

A biblical meal in a 16th-century setting showing the shared dishes for dipping into.

Its simplicity contrasts with the cluttered table of two centuries later.

'depond' (for salad) long challenged butlers and goldsmiths alike. It is no coincidence that many of these innovations for elegant eating have a French resonance. A constant tug-of-war between complex French cookery and 'good plain English food', which at times had political and even religious overtones, meant that cookery writers for English readers had to disguise the subtler recipes and sauces with Anglo-Saxon terminology.

Travellers' accounts highlight differences and innovations. Louis Simond found the English failure to dilute wine with water inexplicable and liable to lead to overindulgence. Catherine of Braganza and her continental successors imported bottled mineral water for the table, although Lady Hervey claimed that river water, even from the Thames, was the best for making coffee and tea. The Jacobean Thomas Coryate was, notoriously, impressed by the table forks he encountered in Italy. Count Magalotti, travelling the other way 50 years later, was shocked by the continuing want of forks on English tables: 'at the conclusion of dinner they dip the end of a napkin into the beaker set before each of the guests … and

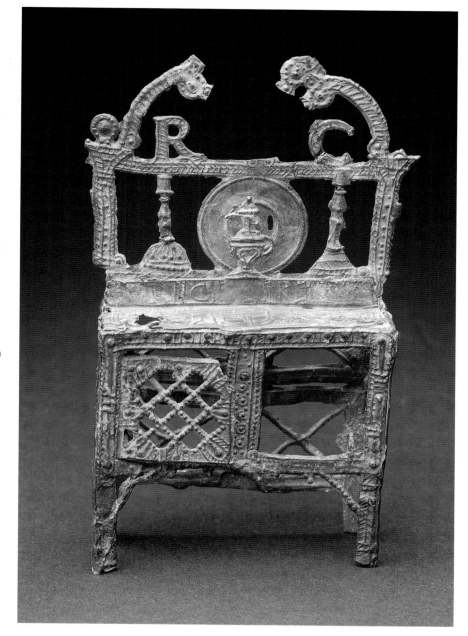

This Elizabethan miniature buffet, with hand-washing equipment above a larder or aumbry, was apparently made as a souvenir of a lavish mayoral banquet in the 1580s.

with this they clean their teeth and wash their hands'.

Forks and their correct usage continued to raise problems. In 1784 Faujas de St Fond disliked both pricking his mouth 'with those sharp little steel tridents … generally used in England' and the way plates were attacked at an English dinner table. 'Not a moment is lost in seizing the morsels of food', he complained, in contrast to the more leisurely French and American practice of laying down the knife and transferring the fork to the right hand. But 'the English are very remarkable for dinners' as the American ambassador Richard Rush commented in 1818. He was struck not only by the mass and quality of cut-glass and plate in London showrooms but also by the pre-dinner pleasures, whether walking by twilight 'Upon one of those smoothly shaven lawns which Johnson likens to velvet', or admiring the 'time-honoured masterpieces of genius and art' in the Marquis of Lansdowne's dining hall.

The study of dining has flourished as the act itself has become simpler. As with early music, there is now a passion for authenticity – to understand the past through research, empathy and direct personal experience. Reconstructed meals are talked about and filmed in vicarious time travel, although without the pleasures of taste, touch and smell. An Elizabethan house, Loseley, celebrated its 400 years in 1968 with a recreated banquet for 100 costumed guests,

commissioning green-glazed mugs from a local kiln for the mead and claret. This evening, by candlelight, included the Tudor etiquette of greeting every guest with a kiss in the fashion so admired by Erasmus. One group of researchers exists to study dining at the courts of Europe, and another holds an annual symposium on food and cookery in Oxford. A spectacular exhibition of silver and porcelain services from European courts, *Les Tables Royales* at Versailles in 1993/4, opened with a historically inspired banquet befitting the setting and attracted exceptional crowds. A bookshop specializing in cookery and food history, Books for Cooks, flourishes in London, and an associated periodical, *Petit Propos Culinaires*, offers recent esoteric research.

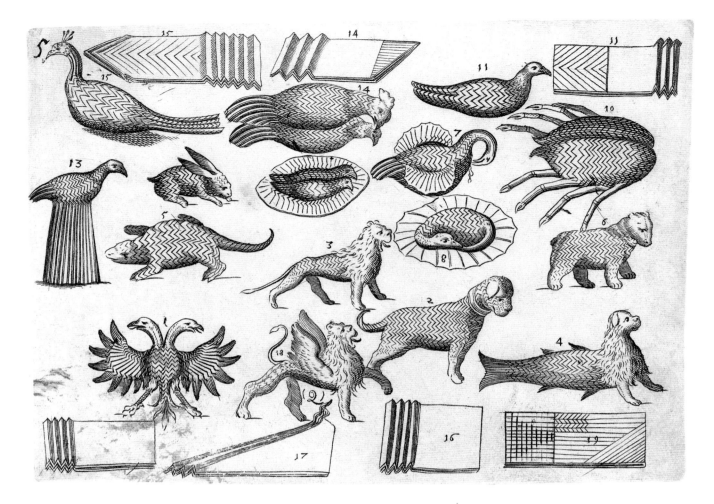

Above: Dining manuals from the 17th century show napkins folded as fantastic beasts. Not for use, these were cleared away before eating or were used as decorations once food was served.

Left: The crammed tables of this ceremonial dinner combine hot dishes with sweetmeats, as in the jellies stacked up for the young prince on the right.

Detail of an interior decorator's proposal for a grand 1820s dining room. Note the apsidal sideboard and alternative designs for chairs.

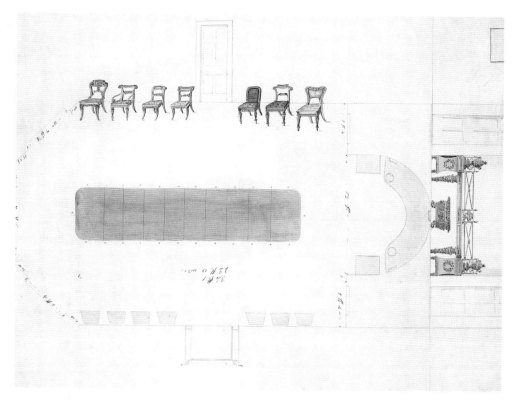

Driven by this popular interest, museums and historic houses are reconsidering how they display objects and interpret interiors. At Hampton Court the private dining room of William III is set out for a 1690s dessert, and the supper table of Princess Caroline is crammed with rococo tureens and cruets with candelabra and glasses ranged on side tables. The evanescent nature of a meal – the fleeting pleasures of taste and talk – is like a butterfly, hard to pin down, but these reconstructions, like the recreated neoclassical buffet at Kedleston, restore meaning to functional objects, which so often die behind the glass of a showcase.

How was all this theatre achieved and sustained? Increasingly people are curious about the engineering behind the special effects of a grand dinner. The archaeology of the butler's pantry is explored at Audley End, and at Osborne House the Table Deckers' Room, a Victorian inheritance from the Stuart court, has been reconstituted. At the Museum Nissim da Camondo in Paris, the late nineteenth-century butler's suite (in a servants' complex occupying several mezzanines) contains zinc-lined sinks and drains, and velvet-lined drawers to protect the silver (his particular responsibility), while the porcelain services have their own glazed storeroom a floor below.

Silver is killed by electric light, which reflects its brightness perfectly and obliterates its subtleties; and electricity's arrival accelerated silver's long decline from supremacy on the table. Porcelain claimed more and more of the table once Europeans had discovered the secret of 'white gold', and more modest creamwares – clean-looking and reasonably durable and decorative – supplanted pewter.

Tableware represented a huge investment of taste as well as cash and it is no wonder that Regency guests were often shown displays of silver and porcelain before dinner, just as renaissance and baroque dinners had been dominated by splendid buffets of gilded vessels for admiration rather than service. When the Drapers Company was left a bequest to buy its first silver plates in 1671, it soon melted down other old-fashioned silver to make up a full four dozen. Each plate was to be engraved in memory of the original donor and they were not to be lent out 'as if they be in Constant use they will soone be battered and defaced'. Remade in 1700, the plates still enhance company dinners today. When Frederick, Prince of Wales, bought two dozen 'Brim'd Soup Plates' of 'Enamell'd China' for £3 4s in 1736, this was a fashionable, less costly choice than the same in silver – £4 plus for a single plate – but enough to pay a quarter's wages for his cook. Today brides' shops flourish, particularly in France, to create classic settings gleaming with porcelain, glass and silver whereas Anglo-Saxon eclectics experiment with Eastern minimalism.

Left: A handsome soup tureen, flanked by a ladle and sauceboat, emphasize the common European preoccupation with costly and specialized vessels for food.

Opposite: A grand North German dinner, where the plate is set out on the buffet, and the table, dressed with a decorative cloth, is left relatively bare.

In 1814 Talleyrand, departing for the Congress of Vienna, advised that the first indispensable item of an ambassador's household is a good chef. He could have added a second, a silver service, borrowed or hired, and a handsome porcelain dessert service. This golden age of tableware is evoked today in the three rooms of Napoleonic dinner plate in the Residenz Munich, the Imperial Silver and Porcelain Rooms in Vienna, and by Luigi Valadier's monumental Roman centrepiece in marble and ormolu made for the Royal Palace in Madrid. London can offer a dazzling gilded buffet and gargantuan cistern in the Jewel House at the Tower of London and the positively princely possessions of the 1st Duke of Wellington at Apsley House. It is difficult in a museum setting to capture the sheer splendour of a large service, since the forms and designs lack their proper context and are greedy of space, but the curiosity aroused in London when Catherine the Great's 'Frog Service' recently came on loan, and the admiration for contemporary table creations commissioned for Downing Street and the Scottish Parliament, show the continuing appeal of the art of the table.

Today we take for granted the idea of the menu, the list setting out dishes in sequence, from which diners choose, but this way of presenting the dinner came only with the arrival of the restaurant in Paris in the 1760s. In dining *à la française*, the great pleasure of 'eating with the eyes' lay in the mass of tastes, textures and shapes set out in geometric order before the guests arrived. By contrast, ordinaries and taverns offered no choice. The earliest 'à la carte' is certainly Parisian, although Boulanger's primacy has been questioned recently. Menus rapidly became an art form, often devised by artists; but in recent years the blackboard with 'today's specials' has become a feature of informal eating out.

Choosing the food is one pleasure, but choosing the company is – or should be – pleasurable too. Today creating a placement is a social skill requiring diplomacy, an excellent memory for personal foibles (and sometimes recourse to *Who's Who*). Attitudes to seating men and women intermingled have varied according to time, place and social group. Historically, those of the blood royal always dined at a separate table and in public two or three times a week, occasions driven by ceremony and providing little comfort. When Christian VII of Denmark visited France and England in the 1760s his formal dinners were notoriously short, less than half an hour (due to his hyperactive personality), which forced his guests to eat and drink at breakneck speed. French and English methods of furnishing as well as laying the table differed: the Englishman played the host in an armed chair at the head of the table whereas the Frenchman sat half way down one side in an armless chair.

Decorating and perfuming the dining room, although not necessarily the table itself, took careful and often costly preparation. Perfuming pans or cassolettes, burning scented pastilles, 'removed the gross humours' emanating from rich and spicy food, and the steward at Knole, Kent, in the 1630s was instructed 'to perfume the roome oftene with oring flower water upon a hott panne'. Attitudes to flowers on the table itself were inconsistent. Until the mid-eighteenth century nature was preferred in its artificial form, chased on to silver or painted on porcelain; the scent of flowers was seen as distasteful in conjunction with highly flavoured food, although desserts featured sugared blossoms as edible delicacies, and lemons and bay leaves ornamented the pyramids of sweetmeats on James II's coronation table.

Hothouses transformed the choice of flowers and the dining room benefited. The crowded dishes of service *à la française* vanished leaving an expanse of gleaming damask clear for vases or complex decorations incorporating the

Fusions of eastern and western design, culinary and dining traditions were at the height of fashion at the turn of the 21st century.

Left: A domestic table setting created by the Hong Kong-born designer Peter Ting.

Right: The supremely elegant interior of the I-Thai restaurant, designed by Anouska Hempel for The Hempel, London.

ornaments and woven silks of the 1880s. In 1897 a guide to female etiquette recommending inexpensive blooms 'better able to withstand the heat of the room and the hot odours of the dishes' suggested Iceland poppies, Cape gooseberries and silver honesty contrasted with scarlet geraniums.

Attitudes to stimulants have varied too. Today, since we dine late, we often prefer to finish our meals with caffeine-free coffee or a herbal infusion. The new drugs of tea and

coffee were instantly popular in the seventeenth century to counteract the effects of food and alcohol and to fuel sparkling conversation when dinner was taken during the afternoon. The drawing room drinking of tea and coffee after dinner was a novel female ceremony, complete with distinctive and costly equipment, whereas tea and coffee pots for more private family breakfasts were plain and utilitarian. Preferences soon emerged for coffee to be prepared in

stoneware or silver pots rather than tin or copper 'which takes from it much of its goodness'.

Old English hospitality – the tradition of offering simple hearty fare to all comers – gave way to a more refined private form of entertaining limited to one's peers or superiors. Eating and drinking, for those who could afford to choose, were transformed between the 1650s and 1700. The dinner service arrived (by degrees) in the same half century, supplanting the traditional ways of presenting food. During the following centuries both dining paraphernalia and table manners became increasingly complex.

This book is about taking objects out of their museum cabinets and placing them back in their original contexts. Drawing on recipe and etiquette books, paintings and descriptions, it explores customs that have died and recaptures a world of vanished pleasures. Enjoy it. (*Bon Appetit*.)

SETTING THE SCENE

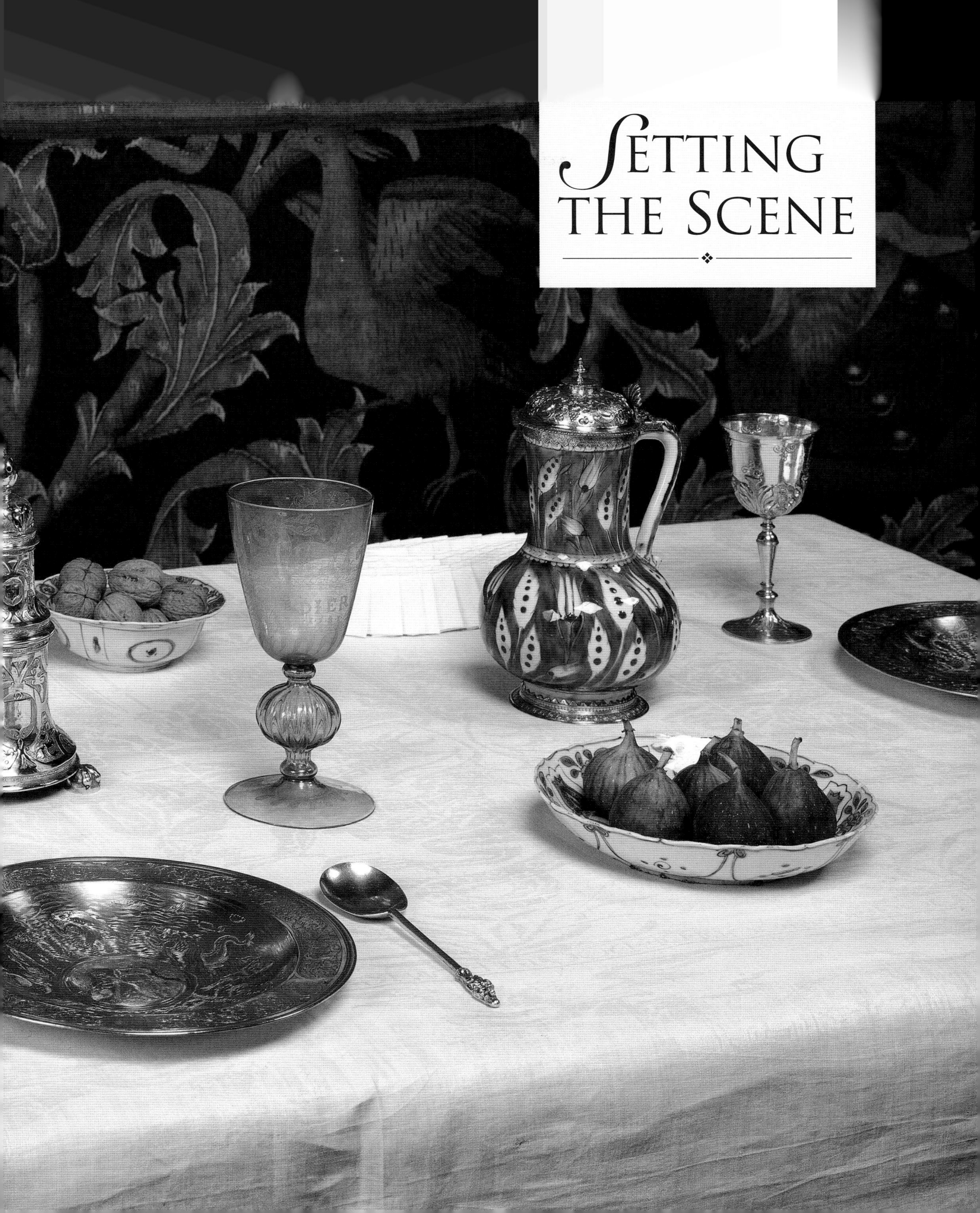

Furnishing the Dining Room

The dinner was served upon a table of [John Joseph] Merlin's construction. No servants attend, but by pulling a bell your plate is pulled down and a clean one sent up; so with the dishes, and all you ask for. In short it is exactly like a trapdoor at a theatre.

LADY HOLLAND ON DINING WITH THE KING OF NAPLES AT CARDITELLO IN 1793

Dining rooms required a range of practical furnishings to be fully functional. Facilities for assembling different courses with several dishes, for keeping food warm and for efficient service were essential. However, they also offered opportunities to display wealth, taste and a sense of style.

Wall coverings demonstrated this combination of fashion and function. In the seventeenth century practical materials such as leather, painted canvas and wood panelling were preferred to tapestries and textile hangings, which absorbed the smells of food. Decorative and elaborate schemes were achieved using such materials as gilt leather, which was particularly popular in Northern Europe. Practical floor coverings, such as Dutch black and white marble tiles, were copied in Britain.

The main furnishings of a seventeenth-century dining room were the 'cup-board' or buffet (see p.22), a table and chairs. Seventeenth-century tables were massive, and had draw-leaves that pulled out to seat more. Folding tables, oval or round, introduced greater flexibility for dining later in the seventeenth century, as they could be stored flat until required. High-backed armed chairs seated the master and important guests, and simpler versions or 'back stools' and benches were provided for others. Chairs were upholstered in a variety of materials, including turkey-work, leather and cane, and were lined up along the wall when not in use. Rinsing hands was an essential part of dining etiquette, in

Opposite: A court cupboard displaying silver dominates the sparsely furnished room. The man alone has an armed chair.

Above: Formality and decorum characterize the furnishings, comprising a freestanding buffet, a set of tables and matching chairs.

Right: Robert Adam combines old family silver and a new sideboard in a setting featuring his fashionable archaeological style.

FURNISHING THE DINING ROOM

both grand and modest households, a ewer and basin – together with a linen towel – being brought from a stand or alcove.

The concept of the formal 'eating room' – one solely devoted to the enjoyment of dinner – evolved early in the eighteenth century. Classical schemes and vine-carved furniture and plasterwork came to be associated with such rooms, where it became customary for men to linger over their wine and indulge in political or philosophical debate. As Robert Adam observed, the British paid great attention to the decoration of their dining rooms, where so much time was spent, whereas the French concentrated on the appearance of the table, not the room itself (which was but one of a series of reception rooms).

In France, food could be kept warm in a servery adjacent to the dining room. In eighteenth-century Britain, practical necessities were often concealed in pairs of urns on pedestals either side of the sideboard-table. One urn would be fitted

with a water cistern and basin, and the other served as a plate-warmer. Freestanding coolers of mahogany or marble were provided for wine, and boxes for cutlery were placed on the sideboard table. By 1820 all these functions were combined in one piece, the sideboard, which continued to be the main item of furniture in the dining room throughout the nineteenth century. The sideboard also contained a chamber pot, usually placed discreetly in a cupboard at one end, and early nineteenth-century visitors to Britain commented on its uncivilized use after the ladies had retired to the drawing room (see p.74). Other innovations included new types of furniture for clearing away after each course. Slotted boxes for dirty cutlery, buckets for dirty plates, and folding tables with trays for dishes became part of the standard range of dining room furniture.

The conventions of eighteenth-century dining did not generally require a large fixed table. Round or oblong tables were formed from sections bolted together, and these would be folded away when not required. They were replaced in the early nineteenth century by expanding dining tables. Similarly, chairs – for which leather over horsehair increasingly became the conventional and practical covering – continued to be positioned against the walls when not in use. It was not until the late eighteenth century that the dining table was placed permanently in the middle of a dining room with chairs set all around (see p.11).

While wooden, tiled or marble floors were favoured for dining rooms in some European countries, imported Turkish carpets and European imitations became general in Britain. These were covered with floor cloths and druggets. Floor cloths, popular in Britain and North America between about 1710 and 1850, were made of painted and varnished canvas and could be wiped clean. In 1818 Sir Walter Scott, the novelist, chose oak-coloured oilcloth to go in front of the sideboard and oak-coloured drugget for under the table in his dining room at Abbotsford, Scotland. Drugget, a coarse woollen fabric, was also used for crumb cloths, which were placed under the dining table and then shaken out. They became quite fashionable in the early nineteenth century, later examples being of linen damask. The later nineteenth

A knife box of the 1770s: attention to detail extends to the classical pilasters and pierced silver fittings.

Left: The romantic vision of the Old Hall at Cotehele, Cornwall, dressed for a tenants' dinner. Family history is emphasized by the Stuart chairs, antlers and armour.

Above: A modest middle-class dining room, with simplified versions of standard furniture and a floor cloth.

century saw the invention of other washable materials, such as linoleum for floors and Lincrusta Walton for walls.

While textile wall hangings were thought impractical for dining rooms, curtains became customary in the eighteenth century. Methods for hanging them were much simpler than for drawing rooms, and occasionally there might be only a pelmet or drapery over the window. Patterned blinds were another means of screening windows, and shutters with sliding mirrors were a grand alternative, as in the Waterloo Gallery at Apsley House in London.

An interest in privacy prompted innovations that removed the need for servants to be present throughout the meal. The invention of a bell system operated by wires, as advertised in London in 1744, was one such improvement. At Holkham Hall in Norfolk, the servants monitored progress of the meal by using mirrored panels on the reveals of the arch above the sideboard recess.

Informal meals, taken without servants, led to the invention of new types of furniture, such as the 'running footmen' of the 1830s–40s, which enabled diners to serve themselves. The dumbwaiter, a freestanding set of circular shelves, was introduced in the 1720s and was praised by Lady Charlotte Bury when dining informally with Queen Charlotte in 1810. In France in the 1770s, all the functions necessary for private dining could be supplied by small circular tables on castors, the top of which contained an ice bucket, and which had tiers

of shelves for plates and food below. At Monticello, Virginia, Thomas Jefferson devised a door revolving on a central pivot, with a shelf attached to one side, which introduced food smoothly from the servery to the dining room. Concealed in one end of the dining room fireplace is a lift that connects with the wine cellar below. In Britain, for after-dinner drinking, decanter and bottle stands on rollers were combined with horseshoe-shaped tables; placed in the central opening, these could be moved about by drinkers with their feet, thereby eliminating the need for servants to be in attendance. Folding screens became useful fittings for masking the movement of servants in and out of the dining room.

Nineteenth-century improvements in communications included various bell systems for summoning servants. In 1838, J.C. Loudon recommended that a speaking-pipe be unobtrusively positioned in the dining room for communicating with the kitchen or servants' hall.

Although the conventional furniture of sideboard, table and set of chairs survived, gradually the formality of the dining room was eroded in the nineteenth century, as such furnishings as pianos, bookshelves, music stands, sofas and armchairs were introduced. With the table permanently placed in the middle of the room, it became the focus of many different activities, and was protected by a thick cloth when not being used for dining.

FROM THE BUFFET TO THE SIDEBOARD

The Presence Chamber had a temporary cupboard six desks high full of gilt plate very sumptuous and of the newest fashion and on the nethermost desk garnished all with plate of clean gold.

GEORGE CAVENDISH'S *LIFE OF CARDINAL WOOLSEY* [SIC], DESCRIBING DINNER AT HAMPTON COURT IN 1527

From Wolsey's lavish display to dazzle the French, to the Duke of Portland's multi-tiered buffet to honour the victorious Prince Eugène of Savoy in 1711, a handsome show of plate was an essential ingredient of a diplomatic dinner, even if the silver was borrowed or hired for the occasion. The principle was simple: to dazzle and beguile. Symmetry was achieved through pairs of bottles and flagons, ewers and basins, vases (but not flowers) and perfume burners – and to plump out the mass, once glasses had supplanted metal for drinks, handsome old family standing cups or race prizes. All these glittering objects were to be admired, rather than handled, a statement of the host's wealth, taste and standing. For three days after a state banquet at Greenwich, for which Hans Holbein painted the decorations, Henry VIII opened up the buffets of plate for visitors to admire.

The buffet was an essential feature of the sparsely furnished rooms used for dining. Whether built-in or removable, they were stepped, the number of stages or shelves indicating the rank of the host or principal guest. When Edward VI entertained Mary of Guise in 1551, one cupboard of four stages was dressed with gold, and the other of six stages with 'massy silver'. But there were functional displays too. A ewery table held ewers of warm rosewater, together with basins and towels for hand-washing; and all drink was dispensed from the cupboard, where cups and bowls stood ready until toasts were called for. A variant was the livery cupboard, incorporating a locker for the daily allowance of ale, bread and cheese, although these were not necessarily set up in rooms intended for formal dining but in the private chambers in which guests spent their time.

Much of our knowledge of the way that buffets were dressed is based on accounts of exceptional royal occasions, such as Francis Sandford's description of James II's coronation, which shows a jumble of drinking vessels, tankards, mugs, cups and bowls ranked on the temporary stepped 'cupboards'. Dressing these impressively was the key to setting the dining scene, at least until the early eighteenth century brought competition from the dinner service. Much of the effect was achieved by bulk rather than beauty or novelty. Charles I, a connoisseur of silver, inherited the 'Great Gilt Cupboard of Estate', intended for use only on state occasions. Its 20,000 oz of silver-gilt comprised an eclectic mix of objects, including spiky Portuguese cups and towering Nuremberg double cups of the early Tudors,

The hand-washing ceremony demanded costly vessels for the warm scented water; these were displayed when not being carried about the table.

archaic water-pots made to the order of James, massive flagons and an Elizabethan cistern. This heterogeneous assemblage so offended the new king that all was sold, much of it ending up in the Kremlin Armouries, where visitors to Moscow can admire buffet silver from the courts of Denmark, France, Germany and Britain.

Until dining settled in one room, around 1700, the serving furniture was not necessarily handsome, nor designed to be seen. The ewery boards set up for lord mayors' dinners or garter feasts were simple trestle tables dressed with damask, for example. But the designs for buffets published by Daniel

Left: In the stark simplicity of the Livery Hall of the Goldsmiths' Company, a niche for plate and a two-stage buffet continue the medieval tradition of display.

Below left: On the two-tier cupboards are bread, clean plates, bottles and tankards for drink and platters for dessert.

Marot show that purpose-made side tables for serving chilled wine and setting glasses on salvers, and rinsing them, were now in demand.

The distinctive seventeenth-century form of buffet with tiered stages was replaced by versions that were built into the room, or that had large cupboards with open shelves, an arrangement favoured in Italy (see p.19). Marble was used for the grandest fitted examples; some French buffets were built into bays that could be closed off; while in Holland and England niches fitted with wooden shelves provided space both for display and for serving. The distinctive Scottish form of this buffet niche, concealed behind doors in the panelling, was fitted with shaped shelves and a hanging leaf that could be raised for serving.

While buffets were still used for the display of plate and for serving wine, sets of wooden side tables, occasionally with marble tops, were used for serving food. By the mid-eighteenth century the sideboard table had replaced the buffet. This was used for the display of plate, for which separate wooden plate stands were provided in grander 'eating' rooms, as well as for serving wine. At Burghley House in Northamptonshire the tradition of setting out display plate – including a cooler, cistern and fountain – on a massive side table, for the pleasure of tourists, already flourished in the 1760s.

Institutions proud of their traditions and committed to communal eating took pleasure in showing off their 'Founders' plate' at dinner. In 1740 the Goldsmiths' Company commissioned a complete set of silver, partly for the table and partly for display. Its centrepiece, a richly modelled ewer and basin supplied by Paul de Lamerie, still presides at dinners, its deep gilding catching the candlelight. Goldsmiths' Hall has been rearranged several times, but the buffet with its purpose-built niche retains its prominent location.

Robert Adam designed sideboards for several noble clients, often incorporating or adapting old family plate, as at Kedleston in Derbyshire (see p.19). Rather more restrained is a side table Adam devised for Lord Mansfield

FROM THE BUFFET TO THE SIDEBOARD

in 1773: of mahogany with a brass rail, this cost less than £30 and was accompanied by two pedestal stands and a cooler. By this time the sideboard itself, like its medieval predecessor the buffet, was solely for display, as glasses were set on the table, and his sketch shows a row of goblets, wine coolers and an urn flanked by open knife boxes. Thomas Sheraton's sideboards also include a brass gallery against which platters could be propped to draw reflected light into the dining room, an effect shown also in Alken's hunt breakfast print of 1824 (see p.107).

A snapshot of Regency interior design, Rudolph Ackermann's *Repository of Arts* appeared each month between 1808 and 1828, its hand-coloured plates showcasing an unrivalled diversity of furniture and interiors. Ackermann comments that the 'form and magnitude' of the sideboard 'render this article of furniture highly useful in the decoration of a dining room', and he often includes a cellaret or wine cooler to match. A well thought-out display was appreciated. At a Washington diplomatic supper of 1817, guests were greeted at the top of the stairs with 'showy ornaments … forming a sort of triple sideboard, the upper platform … decorated with plate and flowers and the lower one contained some very richly embellished dishes … The whole producing something like the effect of a handsome Roman Catholic altar'. The food was 'a most Splendid variety of entremets, confectionery, porcelain and plate'. The Jewel House at the Tower of London held a stock of Stuart furnishing silver that was drawn on and adapted for display, so that a set of silver fire dogs, with the iron bars sawn off and with the addition of statues, became 'Sideboard Ornaments' in the 1820s.

Erected on top of a fountain, this five-stage buffet combines silver and gilded plate with candles to glittering effect.

Above: A monumental Regency sideboard, heavy with gilded ornament, encloses a lead-lined cellaret designed to keep wine cool.

Left: In response to the 19th-century passion for a mass of objects, sideboards acquired shelves and brackets in order to display them.

TIME FOR DINNER, 1700–1890

The conduct of an Englishman's day in London leaves little time for work. He gets up at ten or eleven and has breakfast … He then makes a tour of the town for about four hours until five o'clock which is the dinner hour.

FRANÇOIS DE LA ROCHEFOUCAULD, *A FRENCHMAN IN ENGLAND*, 1784

The time for the main meal of the day was determined by daylight hours and the expense and availability of artificial lighting. In fashionable society the hour for dinner grew increasingly late as the eighteenth and nineteenth centuries progressed. At the beginning of the seventeenth century midday dinners were the rule, but by the latter part of the following one the meal was served in the early afternoon. Lady Mary Coke recorded in Vienna in 1770 that 'whenever Prince Kaunitz dines the hour is very uncertain, and I think it was near four o'clock before we sat down to dinner, but the common hour of dining here is half an hour after two'. Others writing in the second half of the century noted times varying from midday to four or five o'clock, indicating that customs differed greatly across Europe. In 1769 Giuseppe Baretti observed that in 'the Sardinian dominions, from the King down to the meanest artist, everybody [dines] at twelve o'clock; but in all other parts of Italy they dine two or three hours later.'

Baretti and La Rochefoucauld both emphasize the formality of English dinners: 'at four o'clock precisely you must present yourself in the drawing-room with a great deal more ceremony than we are accustomed to in France … you must be well-washed and well-groomed'. In Italy, as in

Above: Single candlesticks bathe the diners and the tables before them in soft light in this painting of a supper dating from 1766.

Right: Five large chandeliers and massive silver-gilt candelabra lit the Banqueting Hall at Brighton Pavilion once darkness fell. Here the diners eat by daylight.

Right: Argand lamps relied on a combination of a cylindrical wick (invented in 1782) and a glass 'chimney' to create an updraft.

France, only the aristocracy dressed formally to dine. Madame de la Tour du Pin recorded that, in about 1789–90, 'we had to be in full dress, even wearing jewels, by exactly three o'clock, in time for dinner'. The length of the English dinner was also considered remarkable: La Rochefoucauld found it 'one of the most wearisome of English experiences, lasting, as it does, for four or five hours'.

According to the French cook Louis Ude, writing in 1836, 'In London, persons breakfast at nine, ten, eleven, and even twelve o'clock and dine at eight or nine'. However, many – including children, domestic servants and agricultural workers – continued to take dinner in the middle of the day. Unless entertaining, city businessmen dined earlier, as they generally worked until four p.m. and expected to dine at home at half past five.

Dining later owed as much to fashion as to improvements in artificial lighting. Lady Mary Coke, visiting Brussels in 1773, recorded 'Since I was here the method of living is quite changed. The Prince and Princess De Storemberg, having

been Ambassador and Ambassadress in Paris for six years, have introduced the French fashions, and it is now all suppers and no dinners, but the hours are much more reasonable than those in Paris.' It had become polite to entertain in the evening, and this trend spread to most sections of society in the nineteenth century, facilitated by cheaper, improved lighting.

Before the 1780s, candles of tallow (animal fat, the best a mixture of mutton and beef), beeswax, and newly introduced spermaceti (sperm whale oil) were the chief source of artificial light. All candles were expensive, and from 1709 a tax on tallow and beeswax candles increased their cost in Britain. Candle ends were collected and reused. As Swift observed in his *Directions to Servants* (1745), 'There is nothing wherein the skill of a butler more appears than in the management of candles'. Dinner services rarely included candlesticks. Made of silver, pewter, brass, ceramics or glass, candlesticks were used all over the house and moved from place to place, as required.

TIME FOR DINNER, 1700–1890

This dinner of 1884 is taking place in daylight, although the table is set with several candelabra. Guests include W.E. Gladstone, foreground right.

The dining room could be lit by single candlesticks on the table, or by an epergne fitted with candle branches (which had the advantage of giving light without occupying valuable space on the table). In *The Cook's Oracle* (1821) Dr William Kitchner recommended 'There should be half as many candles as there are guests'. In addition, sconces and wall lights, as well as lanterns and chandeliers, provided illumination around and above. Provision of better lighting became increasingly important as the hour for dining progressed. From the 1770s candelabra with two or three branches became more common. Dr Kitchner was critical of their effect, however: 'Dinner tables are seldom sufficiently lighted … our foolish modern pompous candelabras, seem intended to illuminate the ceiling, rather than to give light on the plates'. Nevertheless, silver and silver-gilt candlesticks and candelabra were considered an essential part of the most magnificent table settings. Maria Edgeworth describes a grand dinner put on by Lady Spencer in 1813, which had '24 candles on the table in superb branches'. In the early

nineteenth century, candelabra could be bought to match table centrepiece displays; later trade catalogues offered different types and sizes of candlestick, including those specified as 'table' candlesticks.

Despite the competition of oil, gas and electricity in the nineteenth century, candles continued to be preferred by many diners for the special atmosphere that they could help to create. In 1878, Mrs Loftie's guide to furnishing a dining room concluded: 'For the dining table there is no light for a moment to be compared to the soft radiance of plenty of candles'. Indirect lighting around the room was recommended by some authorities: 'It is difficult to have too much light, but profusion is less desirable than arrangement, while a mere glare becomes painful' (*The Habits of Good Society*, c.1859). Shades on table lamps or candles were used to prevent glare.

In Maria Edgeworth's novel *The Absentee* (1812) an upholsterer suggests Argand lamps and candelabra for a gala: 'and of course, you'd have the Sphynx candelabras, and the Phoenix argands – O nothing else lights now, Madam!' Argand lamps, introduced into England in 1784, burned whale or colza (rapeseed) oil; although the oil was expensive, it was found in 1846 that an Argand lamp gave the light of,

Above: The disconsolate couple in William Quiller Orchardson's *Mariage de convenance* take their meal under gaslight.

Below: An Edwardian design for a dining room lamp powered by electricity, introduced in the 1880s.

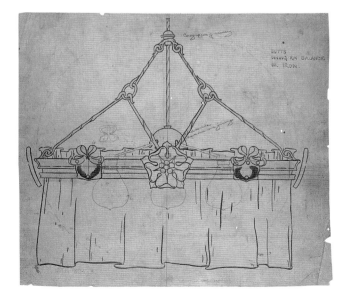

and cost the same as, seven candles. Cheaper oils from fossil fuels, such as paraffin, kerosene and petroleum (which became available in the mid-nineteenth century), expanded the choice of artificial lighting. Mrs Loftie lamented that 'It is not easy to find well shaped lamps. They are generally much too ornate, and made of materials that become tarnished by the oil or petroleum used.'

The merits of oil lamps and gas and electric lighting were keenly debated. Gas was felt by some to be harmful to health, and dirty and damaging to furniture and silver, and although Prince Albert installed a system in Windsor Castle in the 1850s, it never gained acceptance in some circles. As Lady Diana Cooper, reminiscing about Belvoir Castle at the beginning of the twentieth century, noted: 'There were lamp-and-candle men, at least three of them for there was no other form of lighting. Gas was despised. I forget why – vulgar I think.' Early electrical systems, introduced from the 1880s, were cleaner and safer than gas, but they were thought unflattering to women's complexions and to the colours of their clothes, apart from pink and red. The light they produced could be uncomfortable to eat by, one report claiming that diners at Hatfield House were 'compelled to eat their dinner under the vibrating glare'.

COCKTAIL CULTURE

'A dry martini,' he said. 'One. In a deep champagne goblet.' 'Oui, monsieur.' 'Just a moment. Three measures of Gordon's, one of vodka, half a measure of Kina Lillet. Shake it very well until it's ice-cold, then add a large thin slice of lemon peel. Got it? ... This drink's my own invention.'
IAN FLEMING, *CASINO ROYALE*, 1953

The word 'cocktail', used for a drink, appears surprisingly early, in America in 1806. Literally, it describes a tail that 'cocks up' such as that of a cropped-tail hunter or stagecoach horse. How it also came to be a slang term for a mixed drink remains unknown, although it might be significant that cocktailed horses were never thoroughbreds. In 1845 Dickens referred to cocktails in *Martin Chuzzlewit*: 'He could drink more rum-toddy, mint-julep, gin-sling and cocktail, than any private gentleman of his acquaintance'; such mixed drinks were clearly dubious. At the beginning of the twentieth century the short story writer O. Henry described 'A bullet-headed man Smith' as having 'an oblique, dead eye and the moustache of a cocktail-mixer'.

But the decade that first fully defined cocktail culture was undoubtedly the 1920s. In the USA temperance societies forced the introduction of Prohibition laws, the direct results of which were illegal bars and mixed drinks specifically designed to improve the taste of illicitly-distilled gin. In more liberal England, cocktail drinking was fashionable and public. Dangerously raffish, cocktails were distanced enough from exclusively male hard drinking for wealthy young men and women to adopt as their own. They went perfectly with post-First World War abandon, jazz, the Charleston and minimal corsetry.

By 1930, the cocktail barman was a character in his own right. London's Savoy Hotel published some 2,000 cocktail recipes compiled by their own Harry Craddock for the *Savoy Cocktail Book*, one of the most stylish of lexicons, in which he is described as 'the King of the Cocktail Shakers'. The variety was enormous: sours, toddies, flips, eggnogs, Tom Collins, slings, sangarees, highballs, fizzes, collers, rickeys, daisies, fizzes, juleps, smashes, cobblers, frappés, punches and cups.

Harry Craddock, 'the King of the Cocktail Shakers', compiled this 'compendium of Cocktails, Rickeys, Daisies, Slings, Shrubs, Smashes...and other Drinks known and vastly appreciated' for London's Savoy Hotel in 1930.

By the mid-1930s cocktail drinking had spread beyond the confines of wealthy youth to aspirational society, and at the same time it became increasingly restricted by social conventions. The cocktail hour was understood to be a two-hour stretch between six and eight o'clock, and the home cocktail bar was the latest in new furniture – along with the gramophone and the wireless. In 1935 *The Times* pronounced, unchallenged, that 'the cocktail dress retains its skirt about 12" [30 cm] from the ground'. So precise a requirement demonstrates how far the culture had changed from that of the rackety young things 10 years earlier, and how established cocktails were within the social round.

In 1950, T.S. Eliot used cocktail drinking as a dramatic device in *The Cocktail Party*. In 1953 Ian Fleming celebrated it in *Casino Royale*, with James Bond's 'own invention'. In 1964 it was said that 'A cocktail party is the most typical form of contemporary entertaining. Much simpler to organize than a dinner, it ... liquidates social obligations to an unlimited number of people with whom you might find it difficult to carry on a conversation during an entire evening'. The perfect hostess 'wears a dress that is only slightly décolleté, or not at all'. Crucially, guests' dress must 'always be accompanied by a hat'. But the later, iconoclastic 1960s had no time for such joyless strictures and cocktail-drinking barely survived through the 1970s and 1980s.

Then, in the 1990s, came a revival. Flavoured spirits were invented; world travel became commonplace, and familiarity with exotic food and drinks became the mark of financially-mobile youth. Themed bars sprang up in smart city centres and the cocktail was rediscovered. The pressure was on to mix ever more extravagant concoctions.

Nevertheless, romantic history maintains a powerful hold. Recently, chef-restaurateur Gary Rhodes said: 'My favourite cocktail is a Bellini, made with fresh peach juice and prosecco ... it was created back in the Forties as a tribute to the painter Bellini by Giuseppe Cipriani, bartender at Harry's Bar in Venice. You can still drink it at Harry's ... its ... one that always brings back wonderful memories'.

Left: Bordering on the brazen, this naughtily flirty Parisienne entertains acquaintances at the bar: a male view of the independent woman that sums up the more dangerously raffish atmosphere of the 1920s.

Below: Cocktail drinking in Mayfair: by 1939 the cocktail bar was a well-established and respectable rendezvous and a favourite place to unwind for both men and women.

Left: The stylish young man or woman about town required smartly designed bar and cigarette accessories for the cocktail round.

31

SCANDINAVIAN STYLE

Probably the most typical images of Scandinavian-style eating are the outdoor, summer picnics painted by Carl Larsson in the late 1890s. These Nordic versions of the cheerfully informal Mediterranean lunch show comfortable, untidy gatherings of family members (including the dog). In particular, Larsson's painting of crayfishing of 1897 showed the Swedes a view of themselves with which they instantly fell in love. It proved equally attractive to their near neighbours in Denmark, Finland and Norway.

Larsson speaks for his daughter, Suzanne: 'we have to collect sticks for a fire – a red glowing fire big enough to bring the huge cauldron full of water to the boil so that we can cook the crayfish. We spread out the cloth with the great heap of cooked crayfish in the middle of it while Mamma makes the coffee'. The 'schnaps' bottle and glasses are also very much in evidence. Today, the summer crayfish celebration remains a fixture in the Scandinavian culinary calendar but, sad to say, native crayfish are decreasing in numbers and imports from abroad have become the standard.

Once adopted, informality became carefully orchestrated. Beautifully composed table arrangements and traditional

ingredients became a hallmark of Scandinavian entertaining throughout the twentieth century. Perhaps the most celebrated types of meals outside Scandinavia are the Swedish *smörgåsbord* and, even more so, the Danish *smørrebrød*.

Literally, 'smörgåsbord' means 'bread-and-butter table', but in practice it stands for a generous buffet of many different dishes. These are mainly cold, but range from spicy cured Baltic herrings, and cheeses, to warm dishes such as Jansson's Temptation (a winter-warming, heart-stopping dish of onions, butter, potatoes, anchovies and cream), accompanied by ice-cold *akvavit* and beer.

'Smørrebrød' translates as 'buttered bread', but it has become the word for an open sandwich in which the bread, at its best fresh, close-textured Danish rye, is the least apparent part. It merely provides a support for a huge variety of toppings and garnishes. These must be in a balance of flavours, colours and textures, and certain combinations are recognized as classics: marinated Baltic herring; salami, onion and aspic; roast beef and grated horseradish. And, as in Sweden, *akvavit* and beer are normally the accompanying drinks, followed without fail by coffee.

Opposite: Officially encouraged from the 1890s, the opening of the crayfishing season in August is one of Sweden's great annual events and Larsson's painting mythologized it almost from the start.

Right: The Savoy Restaurant, Helsinki, 'a peaceful and light background for the people who are celebrating the festive moments of their lives ... with delicious food and drink'.

Right: The 'connecting link between kitchen and dining-room' from *Contemporary Swedish Design* (1952), a 'Swedish style' solution to modern demands.

SCANDINAVIAN STYLE

The presentation of these foods is often studiedly casual. Woven check or striped tablecloths, wooden platters or boards and stoneware or glass pickle jars are precisely placed, interspersed with artful arrangements of simple flowers in summer or candles ('living light') in winter. Nevertheless, at their most elaborate, the amount of time and care necessary for their preparation means that they can also play a very grand role indeed. A fully-laden *smörgåsbord* is a feast; a perfect *smørrebrød* is a sophisticated appetizer.

The shared history of Denmark, Finland, Sweden and Norway, which has also included The Faeroes, Iceland and Greenland, means that many ways of preparing and presenting the region's foods are common across Scandinavia. Fresh and smoked salmon, berries – cloudberries especially – and forest mushrooms are passionately pursued; spiced drinks from *glögg* to *akvavit* are traditional. Regional specialities have developed as well, of course. Norway is famous for cheeses – the sweet, caramel-coloured goats milk cheese (Geitost), and for Jarlsberg; Finland, with a longer history of poverty and occupation, celebrates the arrival of spring with a wide variety of potatoes, including one named 'van Gogh', and challenges the diner with the extraordinary Vorschmack of Jewish-Polish-Baltic-Swedish descent. A ground mix of lamb, beef, garlic and herring cooked for up to 72 hours and served with a baked potato and smetana (sour cream); it was the favourite of Marshal Mannerheim, first president of Finland from 1917.

One of Scandinavia's most celebrated restaurants is The Savoy, in Helsinki, which opened in 1937. The interior was designed by Aino and Alvar Aalto, as were many of the furnishings; others were ordered by the architects from like-minded contemporaries – the table

linen was by the distinguished weaver Dora Jung. The Aaltos' flower vases and serving platters have become classics of Finnish glass design. The architectural journal *Arkkitehti* commented: 'The acoustics are very pleasant and … the walls are mainly covered with Japanese reed wallpapers. The window curtains can cover the whole outer wall … the matte light-coloured surfaces provide a peaceful and light background for the people who are celebrating the festive moments of their lives at the decorative tables, with delicious food and drink'.

From the first decades of the twentieth century Scandinavian design was driven by social concerns and the belief that functionalism and beauty, properly ordered, would enhance humdrum lives. A careful concern for, and in some cases state-supported research into, the planning of economic working spaces as well as of efficient utensils and appropriate tableware underpinned many of what are now regarded as design classics and archetypal domestic settings. Those key names in Swedish design, Arthur Hald and Sven Erik Skawonius, wrote of the kitchen: 'Beautiful may be a pretentious word for these, yet the good material and design of the equipment – pans, mixing bowls, trays, towels and dishcloths of linen, wicker baskets, wooden spoons – add up to something which well deserves such a description.' The daily table setting was of 'pressed glass in simple designs, or perhaps of faience-decorated ceramics … cutlery … or stainless steel [which] never wears out and never needs polishing … The heatproof earthenware comes to the

'Ruska' tableware, still in production today, is among Arabia's most successful lines. Pots and dishes in which the meal is cooked are an integral part of the design.

Above: This advertisement for Gustavsberg tableware typifies the beautifully composed, artfully uncomplicated Scandinavian style. Table laying with success! (*Dukat för succé*).

Left: Dining area, 1970–2: the designs of the architect Børge Mortensen exemplify all that is most humane and relaxed in Scandinavian living.

table directly from the stove, and so is used both for cooking and serving. The dishes are placed on oilcloth or on a coloured cotton tablecloth. The setting is unpretentious but in each article there is evidence of design'.

Nevertheless, formality still kept its place. As late as 1963 *The Great Scandinavian Cookbook* – an encyclopaedia of domestic cookery containing 'the interesting account of food habits and social customs and those dealing with cheese, fungi, fish and potatoes' – included a whole section devoted to table-laying and serving food, with sample place-settings and instructions on serving with or without assistance. If with assistance, there were detailed specifications as to the waitresses' dress and demeanour; if younger members of the family were helping, 'the girls might wear a cotton dress and a short, white or coloured apron, and the boys …white shirts with a tie or bow-tie'. There were instructions on 12 different styles of napkin-folding.

Formality and classic grace may be perfectly delivered, either relatively modestly at home or most famously on state occasions such as the Nobel Prize award dinner. At the same time, Scandinavia is as much a part of the global village as anywhere. It is receptive to sushi, minimalist presentation, pasta and pizzas, fast-food companies, pre-cooked and packaged meals. Yet a relaxed informality, a comfortable pleasure taken in the presentation and taste of local specialities, and an appreciative awareness of efficient and pleasing ceramics and crisp glass – of woven fabrics and warmly-polished wood, of subtle lighting and of fresh flowers – even now these remain the enduring and particular characteristics of the Scandinavian style.

DINING RESTAURANT STYLE, 1950–2000

Elizabeth David, the first cookery academic, also brought traditional Italian and French cookery equipment to Pimlico shoppers.

Jonathan Swift, who had a lot to say about food, was 'assured by a very knowing American … that a young healthy child well nursed is at a year old a most delicious, nourishing, and wholesome food, whether stewed, roasted, baked or boiled', and he had no doubt that 'it will equally serve in a fricassee, or a ragout'. He should have got together with W.C. Fields, who, when asked how he felt about children, replied 'The last one I ate was quite tender.'

The very knowing American would have other gastronomic pleasures to tempt him now, though whether they are all nourishing and wholesome, rather than simply filling or fattening, is a moot point. Multicultural cuisine has, however, established itself in the metropolitan USA as it has in most other countries. It is not a case of 'the Indian take-away down the road' or 'let's go to the Italian tonight', but of the subtle integration of ingredients and techniques from all over the world into national dishes, modifying here, enhancing there, taking advantage of the enormous improvements in transport and communications to allow chefs complete freedom of creation.

Elizabeth David is rightly credited with having changed the British attitude towards food, opening minds to the acceptance of foreign substances such as garlic (Marcel Boulestin wrote, with forgivable hyperbole, that 'peace and happiness begin, geographically, where garlic is used in cooking'), sweet peppers, herbs – other than mint – and olive oil. In 1950, the date of publication of Mrs David's first book, the generally recognized use of olive oil in Britain was for pouring warm as an ameliorative for earache. *Mediterranean Food* was written to encourage people to 'bring a flavour of [the] blessed lands of sun and sea and olive trees into their English kitchens.' Food rationing still existed in Britain in 1950, but slowly, very slowly, the Mediterranean flavour so beloved of Mrs David became apparent in the country's cooking.

French, Italian and Greek restaurants have been part of the scene in London's Soho for many years, and it was to one of these that one would go for authentic Mediterranean food. The early 1950s saw the arrival, first in London and shortly afterwards throughout the country, of the coffee bar. Huge, chromium-plated Gaggia coffee machines dispensed espresso or cappuccino coffee, and simple food was served – more often than not pasta with a choice of two or three sauces. Young people with low incomes had the opportunity, without going abroad, of tasting dishes totally unlike traditional English cooking, which had become more limited during the 1939–45 war.

Soho, London's centre for ethnic restaurants, was also in the 1950s a centre for specialist food suppliers and a wonderful source of unusual (by British standards) kitchen equipment. A few of the food shops are still there, but Mme Cadec, who owned a tiny shop on Greek Street, full to the

New uses for old buildings: a former West End banking hall becomes a dramatic setting for Chinese food in the late 1990s.

doors with desirable cooking aids, has gone. There you could buy a *hachinette* for chopping parsley or onions and a *bassin*, the ultimate copper utensil for beating egg whites or whipping cream. Mme Cadec was, however, largely selling to the converted; the average housewife preferred newly introduced electrical gadgets.

By the 1960s foreign travel, particularly to other parts of Europe, was much more widespread, and though there were horror stories of coach-loads of tourists taking their own tinned food and copious supplies of teabags – because they 'did not trust foreign food' – the majority of travellers enjoyed novel gastronomic tastes and textures and brought new ideas home with them. The sensual experience of eating delicious food in the warm sunshine fitted in well with the new freedoms of the decade. Many people wanted to reproduce the dishes at home, and a plethora of cookery books appeared – *Balkan Cooking*, *Turkish Cooking*, *Tante Marie's French Kitchen*, *A Book of Middle Eastern Food*, *True Provençal and Niçoise Cooking* and Elizabeth David's definitive *French Provincial Cooking* all gave recipes that required unusual ingredients not readily available outside specialist shops. Supermarkets were not slow to catch on, and exotic spices started to appear on the shelves next to the inevitable – and not very strong – curry powder, which for so

DINING RESTAURANT STYLE 1950–2000

Above: All the elements of the traditional restaurant setting, pared to the minimum, highlight the rich Edwardian pudding.

Left: A table expressing the essence of fusion: Japanese-style food, French bread and olive oil, sea salt and mixed peppers for grinding.

long had been the main flavouring of what constituted 'foreign' food for the average Englishman.

Increased awareness of the pleasures of eating encouraged the opening of restaurants smaller and more intimate than the dining rooms of great hotels or formal establishments; examples included The Ivy or Prunier's, which was run by Simone Prunier with a rod of iron and immaculate results. In London the new restaurants opened in fashionable districts around Knightsbridge as well as in up-and-coming areas. The American Robert Carrier opened a restaurant in Islington, when the early Victorian houses were affordable to middle-income families and long before the district became the home of future prime ministers. Carrier's brought gastronomically minded people to the area; they in turn found, within reasonable travelling distance of the West End, a supply of medium-priced houses crying out for restoration, and the renaissance of Islington was started. Battersea was another area, unfashionable except to the slightly bohemian, but only minutes away from Chelsea, Knightsbridge and Sloane Square, where a looming presence of huge blocks of council flats was modified by the appearance of small but excellent restaurants providing French, Italian, Greek – particularly good – and Tunisian cuisine. More than one member of the British royal family declared their favourite restaurants to be in Battersea.

Just as these establishments brought fashion to certain districts, so they followed fashion in their choice and presentation of food. 'Nouvelle cuisine' – a revolt against the elaborately sauced, highly seasoned food produced by traditionally trained chefs – was by the mid-1970s the order of the day. Carefully and simply prepared ingredients, relying on their own flavour and only lightly sauced or garnished, were equally carefully presented so that the visual appeal of the meal was as important as the taste.

Right: The post-war lack of domestic staff stimulated the invention of electrical equipment to produce restaurant style dishes at home.

A MAJOR revolution

in food preparation by Kenwood

Once the largest garage in Europe, the Bluebird restaurant is one of the the most remarkable dining venues in London – a skylit bar and restaurant, currently seating 260, with views over the neighbouring King's Road.

There were exaggerations – one very smart restaurant decorated each plate of food with fresh flower petals, some edible, some not, which possibly distracted the diner's attention from the fact that, no matter how lovingly prepared and how expensive, there was not a lot on the plate. Some 25 years later the Japanese influence was a direct extension, minimalist cuisine relying on absolute freshness of the basic product and arrangement on the plate to ensure that the eye was as satisfied, or more so, than the stomach.

It is not only in Britain that the delights of multicultural cuisine have become appreciated. There are excellent, imaginative restaurants in the principal cities of Australia,

producing food that 40 years ago would have been unthinkable. Nobody nowadays is surprised by 'blue shelled crab on a mushroom raviolo' or 'fillets of sea bass on a bed of Thai spiced noodles'. A 'risotto nero' is no longer something that only 'foreigners' eat, and, as people become daily more adventurous, there is a considerable market for meat such as ostrich, bison or crocodile, the consumption of which has hitherto been for the very few. As an antidote to such exotica, however, it is comforting to know that a great many of the traditional dishes of any country are still available, prepared with the expertise and attention to detail that is now lavished on more unconventional food.

DRESSING THE TABLE

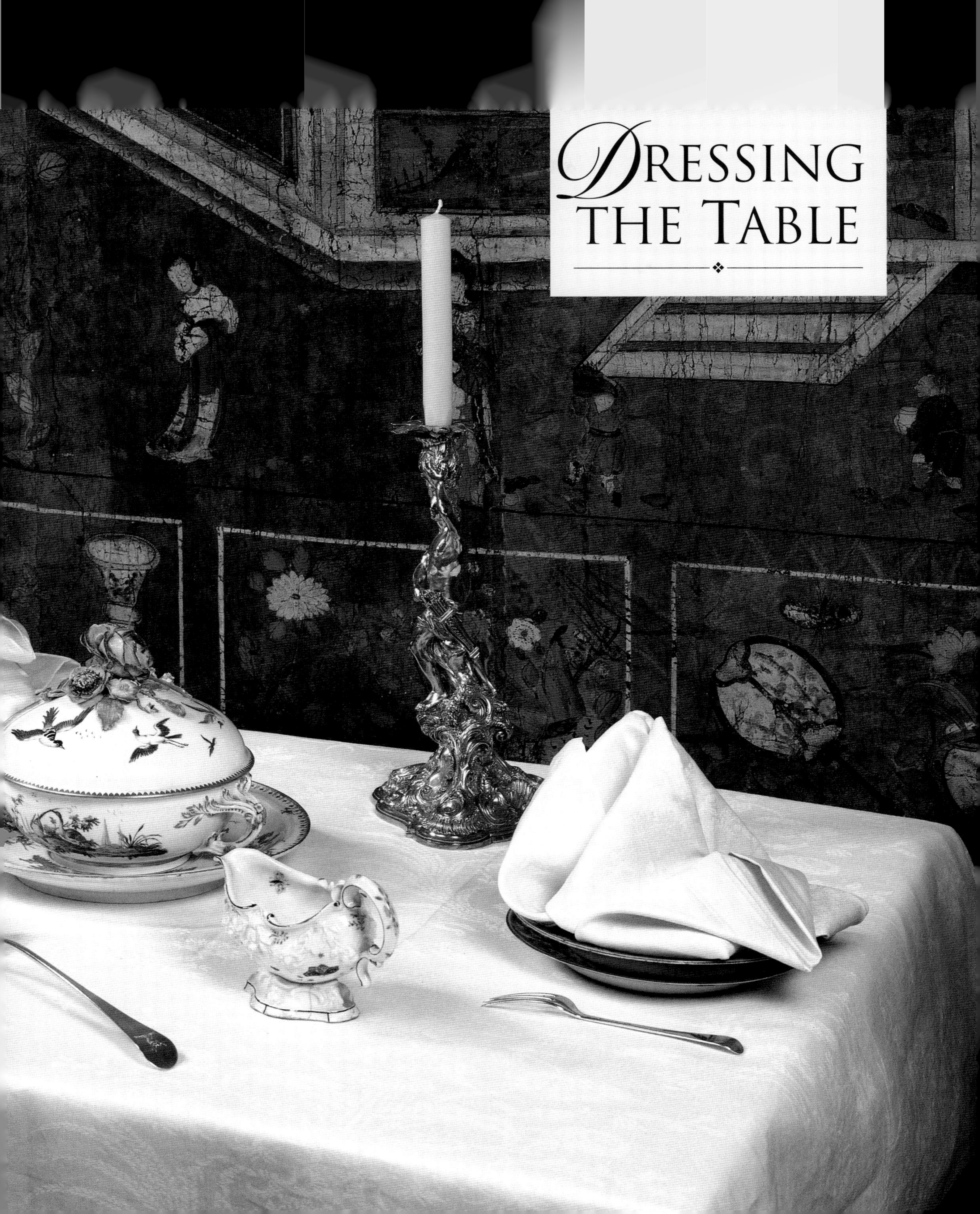

TRENCHERS AND PORRINGERS

Medieval plates were often cut from inch-thick slices or trenchers of wholemeal bread. The word came from the Old French *trencheor* or *trancheur* for a sharp blade. With the crusts pared off, these slices were large enough to serve as a plate, supporting the food and absorbing juices and sauces until the end of the meal. John Russell's *Boke of Nurture folowying Englandis gise* (*c.*1460) stated that the sovereign should be served with a trencher of new bread, while other diners were to receive a trencher made from day-old bread. These were gathered up and distributed to the poor at the end of the meal.

Early Stuart triangular silver salts have their origin in these bread slices. The trenchers were ceremoniously spread with salt and cut up as described at the enthronement feast of George Neville, Archbishop of Canterbury, around 150 years earlier: 'With your brode knyfe take a little salt and plane it on your trencher tyll it be even … cut your Salt quadrant and lay it before your principal trenchers'. From the mid-sixteenth century thick wooden platters, square or round and about 15–21 cm (6–8 1/2 in) across, replaced bread trenchers. Most had large circular depressions to retain the meat and sauces with a smaller well for salt. Prices varied between 4 1/2 d to 8d per dozen. For wealthier patrons, pewter plates in sets of a dozen were available as part of a garnish for a table service, as were silver plates weighing

12–20 oz for the court. It was not until the 1670s, when the ceramic industry started to produce dinner plates on a massive scale, that wooden trenchers finally vanished.

The term trencher was also applied to thin discs or rectangles of beechwood and sycamore of 13–15 cm (5–6 in). These were richly painted and gilded with an elaborate border surrounding a central motif of fruit, flowers (and more rarely figures), together with a posie and sometimes a biblical text. They were normally supplied in boxed sets of a dozen and were variously described as fruit trenchers or cheese trenchers, roundels or 'posie mats'. Unlike their robust counterparts, these delicate mats were reserved for the banquet (dessert) course, the plain sides supporting moist and sticky confections such as candied fruit or wet succades. On special occasions, edible versions made from sugar paste or marchpane were served. In 1653 Peter Stent's catalogue of engravings in stock included 12 sheets for cheese trenchers, circular prints from Aesop's fables, to be stuck on and varnished.

None of the surviving sets are stained with sweetmeat residues, and whilst they may have been reserved as a 'best set', perhaps they had another use. Each is inscribed with an epigram, a sophisticated version of the jokes in a modern cracker, often mocking matrimony, and a salutary reminder to 'Feede mynde with myrth, thy mawe with meate, And eate to lyve not lyve to eat'.

Above: This much-used 16th-century trencher has a knife-scored central depression with a smaller hollow for salt or mustard.

A rare survival of an individual 'trencher' salt of the early 17th century; the shape harks back to the triangles cut from bread trenchers that once served in place of plates.

John Lone Vintner at ye mermaide neare Chearing crosse

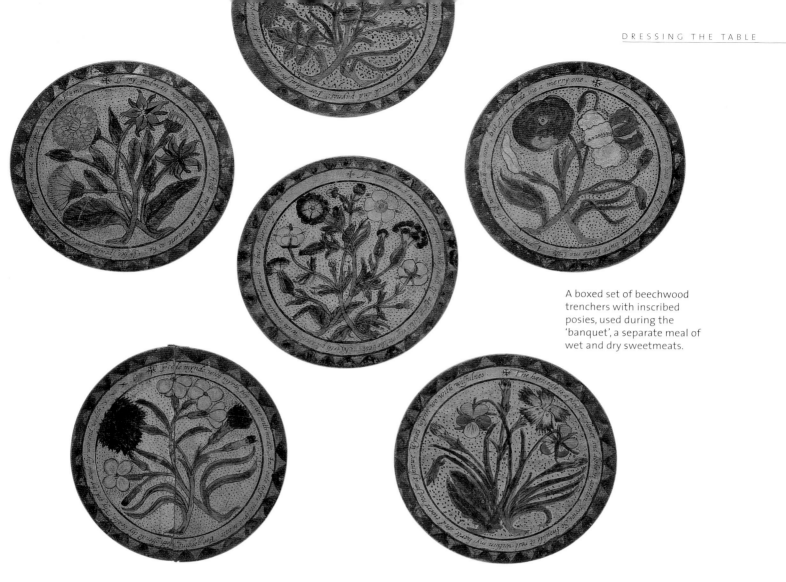

A boxed set of beechwood trenchers with inscribed posies, used during the 'banquet', a separate meal of wet and dry sweetmeats.

A potager or porringer, as it was known in the sixteenth century, is a small bowl made from metal, ceramic or wood with one or two horizontal handles aligned with, or just below the rim. Often described by contemporaries as an 'eare dish', the vessel was an ideal receptacle for pulpy spoonmeats, such as potage, the staple medieval and Tudor vegetable stew, frumenty, a sweetened and glutinous wheat porridge, and pappy milky foods for children and invalids. Randle Cotgrave's *Dictionarie* (1611) translated the French 'esquelle' as porringer, and in 1574 Queen Elizabeth had a gilded silver porringer with a snail on the cover.

Delftware and metal porringers were unsuitable for cooking, but many lead-glazed earthenware porringers have sooted bases, which suggests that food was heated or even cooked in them, set on a chafing dish or placed in the ashes.

Few delftware porringers have survived because the glaze is susceptible to heat and easily chipped.

43

ENTERTAINING BACCHUS AND CERES: CLASSICAL SOURCES FOR THE ROCOCO DINING ROOM

A gilt-wood wall bracket with Bacchic mask similar to one 'for Bustos' in Chippendale's *Director* of 1762.

In the 1750s, when embarking on the creation of a Roman villa at Kedleston in Derbyshire, Sir Nathaniel Curzon wrote a poem to the pagan deities.

> Grant me ye Gods, a pleasant seat, In attick elegance made neat.
> Fine lawns, much wood, and water plenty, Of deer, and herds not scanty.
> Laid out in such an uncurb'd taste, That Nature may'nt be lost but grac'd.
> Within doors, rooms of fair extent, Enriched with decent ornament.
> Choice friends, rare books, sweet musick's strain, But little business; and no pain.
> Good meats, rich wines, that may give birth, To free but not ungracious mirth.

Sir Nathaniel's wish was achieved, since Kedleston's marbled banqueting hall is indeed worthy of the Arcadian deities, whose statues stand in attendance round its walls. His dining room likewise portrays Roman taste, and a bas-relief entitled *An Ancient Repast* is incorporated in its chimney piece frieze alongside griffins, the chimerical fusion of eagles and lions that serve to recall Apollo, hunter god and god of poetry and artistic inspiration. In addition, the concept of 'Peace and Plenty' and the Arcadian paradise of the poets, is evoked by chimney piece pilasters formed as guardian 'terms' or 'herms' with the flower-festooned busts of Ceres and Bacchus. Ceres bears a sheaf of corn, while Bacchus, the wine deity, bears a 'tazza' cup and pine-tipped fertility wand or thyrsus.

According to the poet Virgil, it was these harvest deities who taught the ancients to regain a Golden Age: Ceres by introducing the art of agriculture, and Bacchus by teaching mortals the art of viticulture through the cultivation of the vine. Honouring such deities was considered essential in the decoration of a home, the Roman poet Terence expressing their importance thus: 'Sine Cerere et Baccho friget Venus'. The view that love would soon perish without the support of

food and wine, was echoed by the 'good meats and rich wines' of Sir Nathaniel's poem. Whereas his Kedleston architecture was culled from pagan temples, so the symbolic vocabulary embellishing its furnishings derived from ancient histories such as Ovid's *Metamorphoses* or *Loves of the Gods*.

Bacchus does indeed preside over Kedleston's dining room, where his youthful portrait features in the central ceiling medallion. Bacchus in his youth had been placed by his father, Jupiter, in Arcadia, and it was here that he learnt viticulture from the fertility deity Pan and his merry retinue of man/goat satyrs and their companion nymphs. Since the presence of pagan deities could also be registered by their attributes or associates, so Bacchus later came to be represented by satyrs and nymphs, who gathered in nature's abundance at ancient harvest bacchanals and mixed spring water with wine in large 'krater' vases. Since his triumphal chariot was drawn by lions, leopards or panthers, they too served to register the god's presence.

Likewise Venus, the nature deity and goddess of love, could be represented by her son Cupid and by her attendant Graces. This sea-borne deity rose in a triumphal scallop-shell chariot drawn by dolphins or sea-lions. Flowers sprang up at the touch of her foot on the land, so the shell, dolphin and rose became her attributes, as did the doves that drew her aerial chariot.

Venus, as 'nature' deity, presides over the eighteenth-century French 'picturesque' or 'rococo' fashion. She is associated with the scalloped and undulating forms that provide the structure for the style, whose delightful variety abolished the 'unnatural' straight line. Indeed this 'modern' serpentine line negated the rules of Roman architecture that had been laid down in treatises since the time of Vitruvius. Lauded as the 'Line of Beauty' in William Hogarth's *Analysis of Beauty* of 1753, its twistings were also mocked as 'crinkum-crankums' in David Garrick's play *The Clandestine Marriage* (1754). The Hogarthian taste for 'nature' introduced the ornaments of parks and gardens to the

This massive wine cooler of 1734 was intended to be 'the largest or finest Silver Cistern that ever was or could be made'.

Below: The 'Roman' grandeur of the marble slab is combined with rococo carving referring to the side table's role in the service of wine.

'rococo' interior. Here flowers contributed to the poets' concept of a 'Ver Perpetuum' or Everlasting Spring, and Flora, the 'Spring' goddess of flowers, joined Ceres (Summer) and Bacchus (Autumn) as a festive deity symbolizing a season.

The vine-wreathed cistern illustrated here is formed as a large Bacchic vine-wreathed 'krater' vase. It is borne by love-tamed Bacchic panthers, while its 'herm' handles are formed by a grape-bearing satyr and his companion nymph. Triumphal palms wrap its bowl, which is enriched with antique flutes and Roman foliage after the manner of an ancient 'sarcophagus' chest and displays festive medallions in reeded frames. These reliefs, inspired by antique imagery, depict Cupid attending 'The Feast of Bacchus'. Such silver wine-bottle cisterns lent '*gloire*' to the eighteenth-century buffet, and contributed to the sideboard's 'Grand

ENTERTAINING BACCHUS AND CERES

Appearance'. In addition, the sideboard-table often registered 'Roman' grandeur with a marble top, while its frame might be sculpted in the French 'picturesque' manner. This 'modern' style of George II's reign was well represented in the three editions of Thomas Chippendale's *The*

Gentleman and Cabinet-Maker's Director (1754–62). Chippendale's sideboard table pattern of 1760 recalls the Golden Age by introducing the vine-wreathed head of Pan, Arcadian ruler of the flocks and herds. Pan's companions, the pelt-draped fauns, pipe in the vintage, while its richly

Left: One of the 'very large carved frames ... in burnished Gold, with three branches for candles' supplied by Chippendale to the Duke of Portland.

Above: The bravura carving of this candle-stand features almost the entire repertoire of English rococo ornament of the 1750s.

The Newdigate Centrepiece of 1743 celebrates Abundance and the Elements. Its components can be assembled in different ways for different stages of the meal.

foliated frame is nourished by water issuing from scallop shells. A contented sacrificial goat feeds on its fruit-laden stretcher-tray that is supported by Bacchic lion-paws.

Ovid's history of Pan, and his love for the water-nymph Syrinx, inspired the ornament of one of a pair of gilded wall-brackets that served for statues, busts or candelabra. The harvest is celebrated by the garlanded heads of Pan and Syrinx that emerge from the brackets' volutes, while their herm-tapered trusses are further embellished by bubbled embossments and Pan's water-reeds. Motifs associated with the element of water also provide the theme for a 'picturesque' pier-glass mirror, which is fitted with 'girandole' candle-branches and incorporates reeds in its scalloped and flower-festooned frame of Roman foliage.

Venus's triumph and the element of 'water' are again celebrated in the design of a 'gueridon' stand for a vase and candelabrum. A scalloped tray is supported by water-spouting dolphins that entwine the 'gothick' pillar of this rustic earthen-coloured stand. It is gradually petrified by

dripping water, and while stalactites form on its scrolled trusses, a grotto is hidden in its altar-tripod plinth.

The elements likewise feature on a table centrepiece, whose dessert-dish lid and salvers are engraved with armorials celebrating a marriage. The krater-shaped tureen is wreathed by beribboned reeds, and additional reeds gadroon the pearled ribbon-guilloche of its domed foot. Dragon wings, emblematic of 'Fire', accompany dolphin scales, emblematic of 'Water', which imbricate its bowl, while a bubbled reed moulding clasps reliefs of pastoral vignettes to its sides. 'Air' is symbolized by winged zephyrs – according to the poets, it was the love of the gentle west wind zephyr that transformed the barren earth goddess Chloris into Flora. Two zephyrs, bearing flower-filled cornucopiae, form the handles, and their labourer's hats may perhaps be intended to recall the popular concept of 'Abundance through labour'. More zephyrs feature on the dish and on the tureen-stand, whose trussed legs are borne by festive Bacchic lions couched on 'Venus' scallop shells.

While a poetic analysis can contribute to the better understanding of such curvaceous 'furniture', its principal delight, according to Hogarth, lies in its ability to 'lead the eye a wanton kind of chase'.

À La Française to À La Russe, 1680–1930

When there are but two or three at table, and but two or three Dishes, the Mistress of the House should help everybody once … When there are a great many Dishes and a great deal of company, she should tell them she leaves them to the French Ease, the Dinner is before them, and they are expected to take care of themselves and of each other.

MARTHA BRADLEY, *THE BRITISH HOUSEWIFE* (C.1756)

For fashionable Englishmen, the French court of Louis XIV was the source of innovations in dining etiquette, new forms of tableware and for foods. Indeed, French customs were taken up throughout Europe by the aristocracy and gentry, who increasingly entertained by giving elegant dinners and suppers. In 1660, King Charles II, the son of a French queen, brought French manners and customs to England. English roasts, boiled meats and puddings were augmented by stews and 'kickshaws' (*quelque choses*) – delicious morsels in sauces. The 'French Ease', later known as service *à la française*, formalized the practice at the English court of guests serving themselves. Under this style of service, diners helped each other from an array of dishes within easy reach. In practice, the host and hostess served soups and fish as well as carving roasts, carving being a polite accomplishment for ladies as well as gentlemen. Servants laid out dishes for each course and distributed condiments, drinks, bread and clean plates and cutlery, but otherwise interrupted diners as little as possible; and they generally withdrew completely after laying out the dessert.

Books of recipes and etiquette, from Vincent La Chapelle's *The Modern Cook* (1733), to those of English cooks such as Elizabeth Raffald, contained instructions on the preparation of such elaborate 'made-dishes' as olios and ragouts (rich stews), and how to dress a table to create a colourful and appetizing effect. Three courses were usual at a dinner in the French manner. These are described in William Henderson's *Housekeeper's Instructor* of about 1790:

the first course should consist of soups, boiled poultry, fish and boiled meats, and the second of different kinds of game, high seasoned dishes, tarts, jellies etc. When a third course is bought on the table, it is to be considered rather as a dessert, it usually consisting only of fruits, and various kinds of ornamental pastry.

Many cookery books were illustrated with table layouts. Indeed, laying the table could take up an entire book, as with *The modern method of regulating and forming a table …* (*c*.1750), which contained 252 engravings of table plans. The plans showed round and oval dishes set out on smaller tables and elaborate geometric dishes in the larger settings. It was important to have a symmetrical arrangement offering a good selection of foods to each diner, and the choice of shaped

Above: A royal dinner in public in 1729, showing the dishes covering the table and accompanied only by candle-stands and condiments.

Right: The careful geometry of the layout was prescriptive for both table layers and guests.

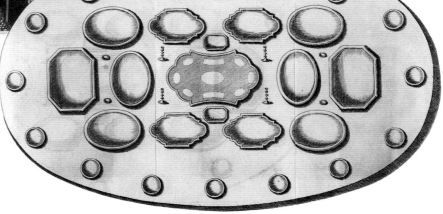

A vivid depiction of service *à la française* with soup, meat and vegetables all set out together, the soup and roast at opposite ends ready to be served.

dishes was dictated by this requirement, rather than by the contents.

The dining table now looked very different from the traditional spread of massed open dishes of the past – exotic, fanciful and costly foods being no longer the sole means of creating an impressive and decorative effect. The elegant arrangement of the new and expensive dining equipment, which the French had developed to serve the new foods, became more important. Eighteenth-century inventories suggest that over three-quarters of family silver was deployed in the dining room, the focus of expenditure moving from the sideboard or buffet, where grand silver for the service of wine was displayed, to the table itself. The new centrepieces, tureens, dish-covers, sauceboats and condiments extended the earlier requirement of simple platters and serving dishes in a variety of sizes. Silver, preferred by the aristocracy, competed with a growing range of materials, including pewter, glass, porcelain and earthenware. The concept that all elements in a service should match in design evolved in the early eighteenth century, but such matching services were rarely purchased in one go, even by the rich.

Although it was during the nineteenth century that a new method of serving dinner – perhaps originating from the Russian court and known as *à la russe*, replaced service *à la française* – experiments in dining style and etiquette had taken place much earlier. Lady Mary Coke recorded in 1767 that 'in Germany one never helps oneself, but every dish at the table is cut up, and a plate of everyone is brought to you'. At the same time, dining etiquette was changing and ladies no longer necessarily sat together with the hostess at one end of the table, but were interspersed with the gentlemen; rank and status continued to determine a guest's place at the table, however.

Unlike service *à la française*, where all the dishes making up a course were laid out together on the table, with service *à la russe* the food was served individually to each guest by servants and the carving took place at the sideboard. Jane Carlyle describes dining *à la russe* with Charles Dickens in 1849: 'The dinner was served up in the new fashion – not placed on the table at all – but handed round – only the dessert on the table and quantities of artificial flowers'.

The English were reluctant to abandon service *à la française*, as it enabled diners to see for themselves the choice of foods and allowed families to show their wealth and prestige in the size, weight and splendour of their table silver. But as English dinner tables and dining equipment

responded to the change in service, silver lost ground to ceramics and glass. A compromise of the two styles of service, using some covered dishes of food, was one solution. Centrepieces and plateaux set with porcelain or glass, and filled with extravagant floral displays (see p.58), challenged the old fashion for silver epergnes; and the cover or place setting, with serried ranks of cutlery for each course, menu card, numerous wine glasses and a napkin and bread, took a larger space on the table. The merits of the two styles of service were debated in *The Times*. In 1859 Benjamin Armstrong, vicar of East Dereham, Norfolk, noted in his diary: 'Had a dinner party on the sensible principle enunciated by some letter-writers to

The Times, and called *à La Russe*. It consists in having fruit and flowers on the table, with wine etc, the abolition of side dishes, and only one dish at a time placed opposite the host. The plan worked very well, and the cook said that it was much easier for her.'

The advantages of the new style of service were obvious to the Victorians, for whom the dinner party was the centrepiece of social entertaining: the food arrived hot, there was less extravagant waste, and servants generally found the method easier. However, dining became more formal and structured, and the intervention of servants distanced host and guest. Moreover, as more dishes and cutlery were

Above: By the 1890s the table was dense with flowers, fruit, candelabra and complex settings with specialized flatware and glasses.

Left: Individual menu cards inform guests of the pleasures ahead since the main dishes remain off-stage in service *à la russe*.

Right: Smooth service was key to an effective dinner *à la russe* since servants controlled the flow of food.

needed for the larger number of individual courses, the expense of hiring servants and equipment restricted how often those on modest incomes could entertain. Society had largely embraced the new method of service by the 1860s, although editions of Mrs Beeton continued to give menus for both styles during the 1880s. The formal nature of dining *à la russe*, and the complex rules governing both the use of new dining equipment (such as cutlery) and the diner's behaviour before, during and after dinner, encouraged the publication of etiquette books. These enabled the inexperienced and those with new money to move in good company.

Napery, 1600–1800

He [the yeoman of the ewery] shall then laye the table cloth fayre uppon both his armes and goe … to the table of my dyett makeinge two curtesies thereto … and there kissinge ytt … after the yeoman of my pantrye hath placed the saltes and layde myne, and my wifes trenchers, manchettes, knyves and spoones, he shall … coverre them wth napkyns.

FROM THE HOUSEHOLD BOOK OF ANTHONY BROWNE, 2ND VISCOUNT MONTAGUE, 1595

The variety of costly damasks found in the linen presses of great houses lessened noticeably in the seventeenth century. As dining became more focused on food and company, its ceremony was simplified, largely losing its political and liturgical connotations. Apart from great occasions of state, when traditional practices continued, cloths such as arming towels and coverpanes fell into disuse early in the century. They were soon followed by cupboard cloths, used on multi-tiered cupboards for displays of plate, which were replaced by flat-topped sideboards covered with small tablecloths. Hands continued to be washed at table with both long and short towels until about 1650. Thereafter, long towels disappear, and towards the end of the century hand towels are listed only among the goods of the middling sort – changes presumably resulting from increased provision of table forks.

Damask tablecloths and napkins were owned in larger numbers but predominantly in the standard widths of three Flemish ells (about 210 cm) for tablecloths and one ell (70 cm) for napkins. They remained expensive, with a set of damask table linen costing in the order of £10 in 1660, the price of a good riding horse. During the sixteenth century napkins had been worn over the shoulder or the arm, but were then increasingly placed in the lap. As skirts became more voluminous in the final decades of the seventeenth century so napkins grew broader in sympathy, reaching their apogee in about 1730. From about 1640 napkins, particularly for *al fresco* dining, could be attached to the waistcoat with a silver napkin hook.

As early as 1550 it was fashionable in Italy to fold napkins into the shapes of exotic beasts. A number of books contained instructions for napkin folding (see p.10). In England after 1660, 'the pinching' of napkins was practised both at court and in the houses of aspiring men such as Samuel Pepys, who paid 40 shillings for his wife to be taught the art. During the eighteenth century tight pleats yielded to ampler folds and simpler designs. Towards 1700, new beverages and the growth in entertaining at supper led to the introduction of tea napkins and supper cloths, although not in significant numbers until after 1750.

Throughout the seventeenth century, damask napery was imported into England from its main production centres in the Low Countries, Kortrijk in Flanders and Haarlem in Holland. The most expensive had designs woven to individual commission, such as those 'with my Lord of Dorchester's armes on them' recorded in 1639 or the parcel given to Henry, Prince of Wales in 1606 by the States General and produced in Haarlem by Passchier Lammertijn.

From the 1670s, large quantities of 'Sletia' damask, woven in Saxony and Silesia were also imported. Certain designs were personalized by the addition of the arms and devices of English families. German imports continued into the early nineteenth century despite the establishment with government support of damask weaving in both Ireland and Scotland. Although there was some early success in Ireland, with the Royal Household changing its yearly purchasing of damask from the Low Countries to Ireland in 1737, Scottish output appears to have been largely confined to personalized products for the Scottish gentry until the nineteenth century.

Stock designs with hunting or biblical patterns made for markets throughout Europe were treasured possessions, handed down in families.

LONDINUM BRITANNIÆ METROPOLIS ET EMPORIUM

THAMESIS FLUVIUS

Above: Designs were woven in the Low Countries specifically for the English market, sometimes with views of London or celebrations of English triumphs.

Left: Early Saxon and Silesian damasks were of poor quality, but this improved after 1700 and by 1750 the most splendid designs were being woven.

Knives, Forks and Spoons, 1600–1830

Forks were undoubtedly a later invention than fingers, but as we are not cannibals I am inclined to think they were a good one.
THE HABITS OF A GOOD SOCIETY, 1859 AND 1889

To the specialist, the term 'cutlery' refers to edged tools, such as knives and scissors, and 'flatware' to forks and spoons. The use of knives goes back to prehistory, while the earliest documentary evidence of the fork for eating appears in an Italian glossary of 1023. It was from sixteenth-century Italy that the practice of eating with a knife and fork in the modern manner was introduced into northern Europe. This development was inextricably linked to the adoption of plates rather than bowls, to serve individual portions rather than dipping into a communal platter. As with most matters concerning taste and fashion, patterns of use percolated via the court. The earliest English silver table fork, of 1632, is from a set made for a noble marriage and found under the floorboards at Haddon Hall, but they became standard equipment for the aristocracy only in the 1670s. The development of cutlery can be tracked in two ways: through the changing shape of blade, bowl or tine and handle, or through the manner of use at table, dictated by a growing number of advice books aimed at the aspirational, and based on an increasingly complex set of rules for polite dining behaviour.

Until the seventeenth century, most table knives were sold in pairs and were sharply pointed for both cutting and skewering meat. By the later seventeenth century three- and four-tined silver forks began to appear, though the two-tined steel fork remained in use, especially for game. In the 1660s the Marquis de Coulanges observed, 'Today everyone eats with a spoon and fork from his own plate, and a valet washes the cutlery from time to time at the buffet'. According to La Salle's *Les Régles de la bienséance et de la civilité chrétienne,* 'At table you should use a serviette, a plate, a knife, a spoon and a fork. It would be entirely contrary to propriety to be without any of these things while eating'. This was published

in 1729, by which date decorated sets of 12, 24 or larger numbers of cutlery and flatware were being made. By 1700 there was also a clear distinction between the table and dessert cutlery, identical in all but size and finish; dessert services were often gilded (and therefore more expensive) to protect the silver from attack by fruit acids. In the late seventeenth century it was still the custom to travel with a personal set of cutlery, to ensure a hygienic and elegant couvert. Ambassadors, equipped by the Jewel House, took sets of flatware abroad with them. William III also took an oyster knife and a marrow scoop with him on his travels, and the latter was often included in pocket sets. The placing of cutlery on the table was subject to variation: in Italy in 1675 anti-papal families put their cutlery above their plate, pro-papal families to the right.

The eighteenth century saw more variety in the materials used for handles – delftware, porcelain, Sheffield plate all being used, alongside cast and stamped resin-filled silver, as well as such traditional materials as agate, tortoiseshell and bone. Around the 1760s it became customary on English tables to place the bowl of the spoon upwards, rather than downwards, which necessitated reversing the curved ends and engraving heraldic devices on the newly exposed surfaces. Many people sent their cutlery to their goldsmiths to be 'turned back' to conform to the fashion. The 1774

Carrying personal flatware ensured that meals taken when travelling would be refined and hygienic.

A 1720s dessert setting. Delicate cutlery is set to the right. The rhyme was an after-dinner amusement.

A 1770s dinner setting. Transfer-printing and green-staining both realized the owner's ambition of splendid effect at comparatively little cost.

KNIVES, FORKS AND SPOONS, 1600–1830

edition of La Salle advised that 'The spoon, fork and knife should always be placed on the right', although the English appear not to have followed this fashion. He added that 'When one or the other is dirty, they can be cleaned with the serviette, if another service cannot be procured. You should avoid wiping them with the tablecloth, which is an unpardonable impropriety.'

When not in use on the table, sets of knives, forks and spoons might be kept in elaborate wooden or fish-skin cases displayed on the sideboard. Lady Pembroke noted in 1732 that 'all the cases for knives … are now made in the shape of a pillar of some order', which she thought 'wonderful pretty'. Robert Adam's designs for the dining room at Kedleston of 1762 (see p.19) show six circular cutlery boxes that are integral to the overall decoration. Letters and diaries of the period indicate the part played by cutlery in the acquisition of a dinner service, a crucial marker of status in society. Cutlery appears early on in the formation of a service, as it was cheaper to buy, and there was no acceptable alternative; in contrast, pewter, glass and ceramics could substitute for

Above: This trade card of the 1750s shows how craft traditions could determine where dining utensils were bought. Here dinner knives are advertised alongside razors, tools and spectacles.

Left: The 18th and above all the 19th centuries saw a proliferation of specialized dining implements. Shown here are (from left to right) an ice spade, pudding trowel and fish slice.

Opposite: The 19th century saw the rise and the decline of personalized flatware, at a peak of diversity in the 1880s.

the larger silver pieces. In 1767 Horace Mann noted that 'Mr Fane's plate cost about £600 to £700 including knives, forks, spoons, salvers, salts and ladles; in short all small things which I have, so that I have plates and dishes to buy'. And writing in the 1820s, the London goldsmith Joseph Brasbridge recalled how one of his less wealthy clients, 'when a young man', had been 'a constant customer … for small articles, such as forks and spoons; for his fortune being limited, he was too prudent to buy anything not absolutely necessary for the respectability of his table'. Even the middle classes had sets of cutlery – the antiquary the Reverend William Cole took stock of his in 1767, finding that some were 'almost worn out: as they have been in daily use with me these 30 years, & as long perhaps with my Father; and my old Desert Knives quite worn to the stumps'. This forlorn service was supplemented by the gift of a case of second-hand green ivory knives and forks with silver ferrules, which must have been similar to those shown on page 55. In contrast, in 1784 Lord Rosebery's cutlery comprised '72 silver handled knives, 47 three pronged forks, 24 four prong forks, 47 large spoons,

36 desert knives and forks and spoons and 3 gilt trowels, 12 silver handles desert knives forks and spoons'.

Cutlery makers included many specialist trades, such as haft makers, spoon makers and knife and blade suppliers. The eighteenth century saw further specialized serving and eating equipment evolve, such as beef machines, asparagus tongs, soup spoons and fish servers. The 1820s saw the introduction of a great variety of stamped patterns with dense heavy ornament, as on the 'King's Pattern' or the later Hunt and Roskell pieces shown here. In the nineteenth century came standardization of usage, and an even greater proliferation of eating instruments. In almost every country the knife went on the right of the plate, the fork on the left, and different sizes of knife, fork and spoon were used for meat and dessert courses. So, by the first decades of the nineteenth century the overall shape and position of cutlery at table had become standardized, the settings only changing to accommodate an ever increasing array of specialized tools for eating, such as fish knives and forks, ice-cream spoons, and cake forks.

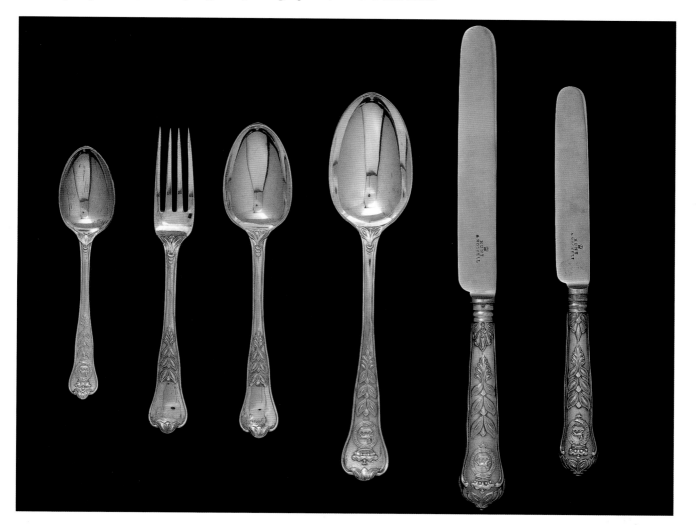

FLOWERS AND GARLANDS

We imagine that before very long no dishes of either fruit, cakes or sweetmeats will be placed upon the table … and their place occupied by flowers and ferns.

THE QUEEN, 1874

This prediction by a writer in a popular women's periodical described a change that was already taking place: by the end of the nineteenth century flowers and garlands would dominate table decoration. This process did not start in the 1870s, however, for flowers, whether natural or artificial, had played a significant part in decorating the dining table since at least the end of the seventeenth century.

Flowers gained their first notable role on the table during the dessert in the late seventeenth century. The celebrated French chef François Massialot confirms the importance of fresh blooms or sugared flowers for decorating dishes of fruit and sweetmeats in his influential *Nouvelles instructions pour les confitures* of 1692. Flowers and garlands were also used to embellish displays of plate and porcelain on sideboards and buffets, as in John Talman's drawing of about 1711; this probably shows part of an 'entertainment' the artist held in Italy, where a tradition of elaborate table decoration dates back to the Renaissance, if not earlier.

By the mid-eighteenth century centrepieces made of silver or porcelain held centre stage on the dinner table, but sugar or porcelain flowers were frequently interspersed: artificial flowers were favoured, partly because the age delighted in artifice, but also because many disliked the smell of fresh flowers at table. Hanging garlands could be used to create dramatic effects without competing with opulent silver and porcelain objects for space, as can be seen from the recreation of Christian VII's banquet, held in 1770.

Flowers had reappeared in a variety of situations by the early nineteenth century. A dramatic increase in the cultivation of flowers took place right across the social spectrum, and horticultural societies, botanical gardens and gardening periodicals all flourished. In this context it is perhaps not surprising that cut flowers became important in

Orange trees, flowers, candelabra and buffet plate set out for an Italian entertainment of about 1711. Note the 'paned' linen below.

table decoration. Early 19th-century silversmiths provided sculptural table centrepieces intended to take flowers, and by the 1860s hothouse flowers were prominent on the dinner table from the start of the meal – the adoption of dining *à la russe* creating more room for lavish displays of these costly decorations. Flower arranging became more formal: careful attention was paid to colour schemes, arrangements of mixed flowers were rejected in favour of themed displays based on one or two species, and conventions dictated which flowers could be used in any given situation.

Potential problems faced diners at tables profusely decorated with flowers. Floral arrangements that obscured the view of diners were an obstacle to social interaction and had to be avoided at all costs, so displays were either very low or very high. John Perkins, an estate gardener, published a series of designs for elaborate low-level table decoration in 1877. He recommended a system whereby cut flowers were laid directly on the tablecloth. A vast quantity of freshly cut flowers would have been required to maintain a decorative scheme such as this – Perkins suggests that five designs a week would be required in 'large establishments'.

Bedford Lemere's photograph of an extravagantly

John Perkins' design of 1877 for a floral arrangement for a breakfast is reminiscent of a formal garden plan.

A reconstruction of a royal dinner of 1770 based on the unusually complete records of the Marshall of the Danish court. The grandeur is relieved by swags of fresh flowers and the sound of water in the marble fountain.

A taste for palms, ferns and grasses, drawing on the richness of the conservatory, was a feature of late Victorian and Edwardian dining.

decorated private supper table at the Savoy illustrates the density of vegetation acceptable on and around the table in the last years of the nineteenth century. By 1910 one author could argue that the disappearance of mirrors, epergnes, ribbons and other 'abominations' demonstrated that the 'science of Floral Decoration in England had made more rapid progress than … any other art'. His confident statement indicates the importance of flowers in contemporary table decoration and hints at the dominance of the professional florist, who could dress the table with flowers and even co-ordinate floral colour schemes to match the dress of the hostess and guests.

'Saucers', Casters and Tureens, 1600–1800

Some furniture of the household of this mettall [pewter] as we commonly call by the name of vessell is sold usually by the garnish, which doth contain twelve platters, twelve dishes, twelve saucers.

WILLIAM HARRISON, *DESCRIPTION OF ENGLAND*, 1586

Until about 1700 the grander the dinner, the harder it was to enjoy food that was both hot and tasty. The savour of a sauce, the delicate aroma of a soup, the piquancy of ketchup and dressing for a salad, all demanded implements designed for the purpose, whether to retain the heat or dispense. Covers to seal in flavour, cruets for oil and vinegar, sets of casters for pepper mustard and sugar are all refinements that crept northwards from Italy, to be followed onto the table by their more weighty companion, the tureen or '*soupière*'.

The 'saucers' of the Elizabethan description were simple shallow dishes set out among larger platters for dipping morsels of bread or meat. Something deeper with two handles and two spouts, 'avec deux anses et deux becs' as the *Mercure de France* described this innovation in the 1690s, was devised for Louis XIV's table and rapidly taken up. By the 1740s rococo fantasies for serving sauces included boats resting on dragons, chased with lampreys, or even cast from actual crabshells. These playful objects remained on the table and were handled by diners, so meriting their costly details and matching ladles. As for the service of the dessert, many patrons preferred the delicate confections created at Meissen, Sèvres or Chelsea, since porcelain 'boats' were less costly than silver and had the added attraction of colour. According to André Rouquet, writing in the early 1750s, the English decorated their tables with 'only a few pieces of plate', a 'choice collection of porcelane' supplying 'the place of a richer service'.

Before casters arrived, standing salts were often crowned by a 'sprinckle' or shaker for spices. Sugar, a luxury, needed no container, as it came onto the table only as part of the dessert or in a box accompanying wine. A set of casters was a fitting novelty to give a Jacobean nobleman at New Year, perhaps following the Spanish, who had already adopted stands for condiments and casters. In the 1630s the Dutch East India Company sent wooden models for casters and mustard pots or 'cups' to China as patterns for export porcelain; and Lady Brilliana Harley sweetened her son's Oxford landlady with a gift of Chinese porcelain casters – fragile rarities – in a parcel that he was instructed not to open. But the concept of three casters – the largest for sugar, flanked by a pair for black or red pepper and dry mustard, and often termed a 'Box' and sold with a spoon – arrived in London only in the 1670s.

Cruets for oil and vinegar to dress salads, double flasks of maiolica, or glass imported from Italy, came onto the English table a little earlier; the Earl of Northumberland owned silver 'salet' plates in the 1620s, and 'potherbs' were a regular side dish. Indeed, John Evelyn dedicated an entire book, *Acetaria*, to dressings and ingredients for salads in the 1690s. As part of the French royal goldsmiths' formalization of the tableware of Louis XIV, cruets, casters and that longstanding element, the spice-box with its integral nutmeg grater, were tidied onto the centrepiece, as depicted by François Massialot (see p.66). However, competition for table space from tureens and candelabra, the inelegance of stretching for seasonings, and the larger choice of flavoured vinegars, anchovy sauces and ketchups drove the stands for cruets and casters to the sideboard. These were brought from the sideboard by servants when required, only the small salts remaining on the table: 'However handsome a cruet

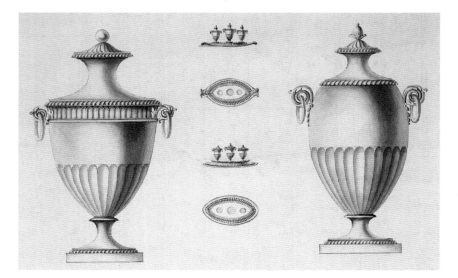

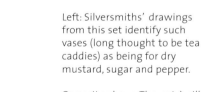

Left: Silversmiths' drawings from this set identify such vases (long thought to be tea caddies) as being for dry mustard, sugar and pepper.

Opposite above: The *pot à oille* of France was for 'olla', a Spanish stew of meat and vegetables, but was used also to serve whole game birds steeped in aromatic juices.

Opposite below: Devised to please the hands and eyes of Regency diners, these richly encrusted sauce tureens draw on William Kent's architectural designs of the 1740s.

'Saucers', Casters and Tureens, 1600–1800

stand may be, it should never be placed on the dinner table
… its proper place is the sideboard', emphasized a late
Georgian etiquette book.

The word 'tureen', French in flavour, does not appear in
Louis XIV's silver inventories, although his goldsmiths
created new vessels for both soup and ragout, which we
consider the origin of these important items. Their need
sprang from the increasingly refined use of ingredients and
the emphasis on delicately seasoned sauces; a terrine for
'viands cuit en sauce' was first described in 1673. At the
same time it became fashionable to serve a bouillon at the
beginning of dinner, demanding a new serving vessel, the
'Soupe Dishe'. Quite rapidly a deeper plate for soup
supplanted the ancient single portion *ecuelle* of the French
or pottinger of the English, although the French kept a
distinct preference for serving a small quantity of a
concentrated flavourful bouillon or *jus* in a covered cup.

As with the terms 'mazarine' or 'intermesse' of the 1670s,
tureen is an Anglicism, first occurring around 1700, which

honours France as the perceived source of a new kind of
menu, since the latest recipe books, the most fashionable
chefs and the most skilful silversmiths were French.
Ambassadors to France were quick to adopt these new
ways of dining, borrowing tureens, epergnes, sauceboats
and shaped dishes for entremets from the Jewel Office,
whose records testify to their rapid adoption by the
English aristocracy.

Today two distinct vessels are classed as tureens, objects
that the French chef Vincent La Chapelle was careful to
distinguish in his manual of 1733. A round vessel, called in
William III's inventories a 'Soupe Dishe', set up on legs and
with prominent, often heraldic, handles, 'opened' the first
course. Removed after the host or hostess had served all
guests, it was accompanied on the table by sets of lower, but
large and heavy covered vessels, La Chapelle's 'Terrine or
Olio'. These had matching underdishes and were often
decorated with fish, game or vegetables, celebrating their
delicious contents. So essential were these handsome vessels

Cruet stands, like
breadbaskets, were brought to
the table when called for.
Offering this massive
condiment stand took two
hands.

Novelty condiments were popular as a talking point. Like mustard pots, they were not required to match the design of the service.

Below: An art deco caster: each wave of 20th-century design demanded fresh solutions to presenting condiments that looked fashionable, a practice continued by the Goldsmith's Company and Crafts Council to this day.

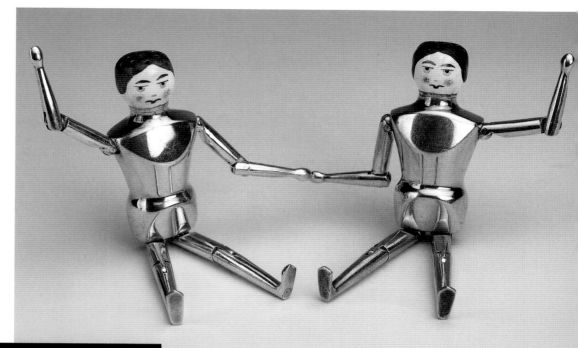

to the French noble table that when Louis XIV banned the lavish use of silver for dining (to ensure a flow of bullion to finance his wars), Parisian goldsmiths invented a new term, '*marmite*', to evade his prohibition.

Apart from some astonishing rococo examples ordered from abroad, these inventive French tureens are known only through designs, paintings and English versions. A pair with the mark of the Huguenot Paul de Lamerie, probably made for the gourmet Earl of Chesterfield in the mid-1730s, are encrusted with ingredients for a delicious winter stew: beet, turnip, curly kale, a woodcock, partridge, rabbit, boar and mutton. A tureen of this complexity was a costly purchase, since it was not only heavy (at 150 oz or more), but also time-consuming to cast and chase; at up to 13 shillings per ounce, the fashioning charge made a pair of tureens more expensive than a Gainsborough portrait.

Tureens kept their value, and many from the 1730s onwards have been preserved, particularly those with appealing decoration. George III was pleased to acquire second-hand a massive neoclassical pair made in Paris for the Neapolitan Ambassador, which stand to the fore in the view of the Gothic Dining Room at Carlton House (see p.118), and which still appear at Buckingham Palace dinners. Lavish displays of tableware were much admired in the 1820s and 1830s, and both the Prince Regent and the Duke of Wellington set up porcelain and plate rooms for their guests to view before dinner, and found it natural to praise the craftsmanship and inventive design of their respective services.

FROM THE SALT TO THE CENTREPIECE, 1580–1780

Protocol and fashion governed the dressing of the dining table, the stage for the rituals of the dinner. Nowhere is this more apparent than in the way the salt evolved into the centrepiece. From the fourteenth century the standing salt presided over the table; from the seventeenth century, following the Parisian fashion, the standing salt was gradually ousted by the centrepiece. This was not because salt had ceased to be a table necessity, but because society demanded a novelty that reflected more complex etiquette and table dining practices.

A renaissance salt continuing the medieval tradition of allowing splendour and symbolism to override the practicalities of seasoning food.

Salt had long been a highly prized commodity enveloped in tales of its life-giving properties, a symbol of immortality and incorruptibility. Although it was widely available, the methods of extraction and refining salt were laborious and costly. Large open pans of brine were set over fires to boil and evaporate: if the water simmered slowly coarse-grained salt resulted; if the bubbling was vigorous, the salt was fine. Packed into moulds, fine-grained salt was stored until it dried into solid 'lumps' to be broken down for use in the kitchen or at table. These processes, combined with the monopolies and taxes that controlled them, made salt an expensive necessity.

Medieval custom demanded that such an important condiment should be presented in a suitably grand and expensive vessel. The focal point of the table, this ceremonial object was made in silver gilt, white silver or pewter, depending on the owner's wealth; it was the single large and decorative item on the table, although smaller 'trencher' salts were also provided. A small quantity of salt was placed into the central depression of the great salt, which was covered to give symbolic protection of its precious contents.

The Vyvyan Salt, shown here, is mannerist in style and monumental in scale, standing over 40 cm ($15\,^3/4$ in) high. The painted glass panels (*verre eglomise*) set into the silver-gilt cover and body make it a unique survival, although there is documentary evidence for similar pieces, including several described in Queen Elizabeth's inventory of 1574. Ownership of such a magnificent and fashionable salt was a tangible demonstration of the owner's taste and stature, and it contained visual messages for his well-educated guests. Surmounted by a figure of Liberty holding her attributes, a sword and a pair of scales, the salt was a symbol of the power and fair hand of the Vyvyan family. The intricately painted panels warn against the dangers of excess and greed in body and spirit.

As fashions and consumer demands changed, so did the salt cellar. The Moody Salt, with its waisted body, 'arms' or branches, chased leaf decoration and paw feet, features decorative techniques and ornament fashionable in the 1660s. Silversmiths from overseas, such as Wolfgang Howzer, who made the Moody Salt, were encouraged to come to England with designs and techniques perfected at other European courts.

The four scroll arms on this piece reflect its composite nature, devised in Paris in the 1620s. Abraham Bosse's engraving of about 1630 shows the table clear of the serving vessels and dominated by the centrally placed salt, which remained in place until after the dessert. In 1651 the Earl of Derby had a great salt with three branches that could be used as candlesticks. This was a transition point in the evolution of a new object – the centrepiece – on which

Above: A fashionable salt dominates this French table of the 1630s, otherwise set only with plates. The women are cooking apple fritters.

Right: The Moody Salt, with its scroll supports, represents an early stage in the evolution of the salt into the centrepiece.

combined together in a single frame, gaining independence from the surtout. Salts, now smaller, less decorative, and made in matching sets, were evenly distributed around the table, one to two diners.

Until the early eighteenth century the silversmith had ruled over the truly fashionable table, apart from the dessert, which might be served on Chinese porcelain, amber, hardstone, painted glass or other precious materials. The opening of the Meissen factory in 1710, with its closely guarded secret recipe for hard-paste porcelain, introduced silversmiths to their first real contender for supremacy. The Meissen centrepiece on page 67 here exemplifies the exuberance and fanciful nature of the rococo. Equipped with sugar caster, cruets and mustard jar, it supports little food. The central basket was perhaps intended to display an exotic fruit or flowers, and the small baskets carried by figures may

delicacies could be displayed throughout the meal, which could incorporate candle-branches, and in which the combination of function and ornament became the focus of attention at table. In 1661 Samuel Pepys recorded that the Queen, Catherine of Braganza, was to be given 'a salt-sellar of silver, the walls christall, with four eagles and four greyhounds standing up at the top to bear up a dish', a form new to him, which he thought 'one of the neatest pieces of plate' he had ever seen. Its successor, the 'surtout' or centrepiece, was to become the heart of an integrated dinner service, setting the decorative theme for the wealth of tureens, sauceboats, condiments, dishes, and plates that surrounded it.

The woodcut from François Massialot's *Le Nouveau cuisinier royal et bourgeois* (1716 edition), shown overleaf, is the earliest illustration of such a surtout-type centrepiece. In essence the early centrepiece for the first removes was a complex object capable of being used in several ways. The decorative tray carried a central tureen, surrounded by the sugar casters, cruets, spice boxes and trencher salts required to enhance the *ragout* or soup it contained. These centrepieces, which reached a peak of inventiveness between the 1730s and the 1760s, were often fitted with candle-branches – important since dinner could last for several hours, and supper was a night meal. Constantly in the eighteenth century, new shapes were evolving for the containers for condiments, which were often

65

FROM THE SALT TO THE CENTREPIECE, 1580–1780

have been filled with comfits for the guests. Although the overall design and colouring might suggest the centrepiece was intended for the dessert, the bottles contained condiments for the savoury courses.

The centrepiece remained on the table throughout the savoury courses and was only removed, if at all, for the dessert. If it remained on the table, it might be modified by substituting alternative branches and dishes; if removed, it was replaced by another, often more elaborate in design, supporting baskets or shallow bowls filled with sweetmeats, jellies, creams, and fresh or candied fruit. English goldsmiths and butlers called these elaborate structures 'epergnes' (as well as 'aparns', 'Save Alls' and 'Machines'), a term unknown in France but expressing their nature as 'treasuries', saving trouble for servants, and bringing everything precious together. The silver example of the 1760s shown here is dressed with fruits that imitate in size, shape and colour those of the eighteenth century. As with the Meissen example, such centrepieces were designed to dominate the table, without matching dishes. The nature of their ornament enabled them to fit happily with other tablewares, whether ceramic, glass, silver or even architectural confections made of sugar.

Above: An epergne of the 1760s, dressed with fruit, which dispenses with the tureen and condiments of the early surtout.

Below: Massialot's woodcut of an early surtout, complete with tureen, condiments and candle-branches. The Newdigate Centrepiece of 1743 (see p.47) shows how it developed.

Opposite: This towering Meissen centrepiece exploits the novelty of porcelain, placing practical requirements secondary to aesthetic effect.

FOUR HUNDRED YEARS OF KEEPING FOOD HOT

Left: This decorative and massive cover of silvered brass was one of a set supplied to Charles Howard, 3rd Earl Carlisle.

Opposite top: Three solutions to the challenge of keeping food warm, two of which relied on hot water – the argyle and hot water plate (centre and right) – and the third on a heated iron block (left).

Opposite bottom: Dish-crosses with spirit lamps elevated serving vessels at table while keeping their contents warm.

To the readers of Robert May's *The Accomplisht Cook* (1660), observing the instruction to serve up a dish 'hot to the table' was no inconsiderable feat, as options for keeping food warm – both before it arrived at the table and once upon it – were distinctly limited in the seventeenth-century household.

The typical arrangement, from the late seventeenth-century, of hot alongside cold dishes acknowledged this difficulty, for periodic 'removes' enabled the table to be refreshed with dishes brought direct from the kitchen hearth. Yet even then, the complex rules of service at such meals meant that uncovered dishes were often quite cold by the time all guests had partaken. While this mode of dining endured into the nineteenth century, the changing surroundings and etiquette of formal eating demanded methods of keeping food hot.

Covering dishes before bringing them to the table was a simple, time-honoured solution. Medieval cooks had adopted the device of inverting one dish over another and sending them to the table wrapped in a napkin: the fourteenth-century author of the *Ménagier de Paris* thought it a great privilege to be served with covered dishes in this way. Shaped, especially domed, metal covers for serving dishes

and platters, which served a similar function, were a late seventeenth-century innovation. From the tin covers in the 1723 inventory of John Beecroft, a Norwich coachman, to the exhaustively-equipped kitchens of the Royal Pavilion, they were to be found in many households and many materials, including tinned iron, pewter, silvered brass, Sheffield plate and silver. Covered dishes certainly kept food hot, but they also retained the resulting steam. The swift upwards flick of the wrist that kept the condensed steam inside the cover, rather than allowing it to drip over the neighbouring guests, was a skill all aspiring footmen needed to acquire and perfect.

Servants' manuals reveal that such dish covers only kept food warm until placed upon the table. Thomas Cosnett advised in *The Footman's Directory and Butler's Remembrancer* (third edition, 1825), that once all the dishes in a remove had been uncovered, the covers should be taken from the dining room. At this point, table-top warming was required. Perhaps most widely available, and simplest to use, was the hot-water plate, with its built-in reservoir for boiling water. These dishes – fashioned from pewter, brass, Sheffield plate and silver, as well as porcelain – were common from the late eighteenth century. Amongst its essential kitchen

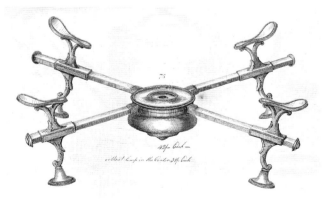

paraphernalia, the 1890 edition of *Beeton's Every-day Cookery and Housekeeping Book* illustrated a metal hot-water plate little different from its eighteenth-century predecessors. Metal tureen-liners without soldered seams were another solution to this problem. These could take the heat of the ranges used in large Georgian kitchens and keep food warm until the tureen came to the table, and they had the further advantage of protecting costly porcelain from thermal shock.

At once ornamental and practical, dish-crosses were also desirable furnishings for the eighteenth- and early

nineteenth-century dining table. Intended as a means of keeping hot dishes from marking the table surface, and of raising dishes to handsome effect, they were adapted for warming by the addition of a small oil or spirit lamp. By 1800, such lamps were fitted with diffusers to distribute the heat across the surface of the dish and so prevent food from being scorched. With decorative detailing quickly adaptable to shifting stylistic demands, dish-crosses fitted out British and colonial tables *à la mode*, as an advertisement in the *Philadelphia Gazette* of 15 December 1763, for the latest 'imported ex's with sliders and lamps for dishstands' indicates.

Insulation and direct heat were applied to an ever-widening variety of goods to ensure food was served forth hot. The Regency table might be adorned with covered porcelain tureens and vegetable dishes, dish-crosses and lamps, and specialized utensils such as the argyle, a double-walled lidded pot for keeping gravy at the correct temperature. The use of Sheffield plate and other precious metal substitutes made such goods affordable for 'middling' as well as noble tables and sideboards.

Yet it was the aristocratic household that most needed ingenious responses to this problem. As the eighteenth-century country house covered ever more square-footage,

FOUR HUNDRED YEARS OF KEEPING FOOD HOT

and the distances servants had to cross between kitchen and dining room lengthened, designers and architects incorporated facilities for food-warming. The elaborate plate warmer designed for the Northumberlands at Kedleston was not only 'extremely handsome' (the Duchess' own description), but it would also have heated numerous dinner plates while the food travelled from the separate kitchen pavilion to the state dining room. At Uppark in Sussex, it was probably Humphrey Repton who designed, around 1810, a tunnel between the separate service block and the main house. Servants wheeled charcoal-heated or hot-water-insulated cupboards through the tunnel to the servery, which Repton also designed, where a heating closet was installed.

Technological developments in the kitchen – including the adoption of ranges with in-built hot-closets and bains-marie for keeping delicate foods warm – and changing ideas about both the format of dinners and the potential dangers of ill-prepared food, all underpinned the increasingly strident call of nineteenth-century household manuals that dinners should be served forth 'deliciously hot'. The declining numbers of domestic servants in households was to be no impediment to this. As *Beeton's Every-day Cookery and Housekeeping Book* urged, 'the viands, if hot ones, [must] be served *really* hot, and with *really* hot plates, and let there be as little delay as possible between the courses'.

Towards the close of the nineteenth century, in the face of the 'servant problem', alternatives to the formal dinner flourished. Central to the success of supper parties was the chafing dish. Classical in origin, and indeed one of the few implements available for cooking and warming food in an age before kitchens became universal, the chafing dish was revived as part of a reaction to the length of, and elaborate preparations needed for, dining *à la russe* or *à la française*. The chafing dish also reflected a new tone in domestic hospitality: 'the highest honour a host can confer upon a guest [is] to prepare food for him with his own hands', the author of *One Hundred Recipes for the Chafing Dish* (1894) observed.

While the advent of gas and electricity – which became almost-universal domestic utilities by the middle of the twentieth century – transformed home cookery, so changing work-patterns and social mores reconfigured domestic hospitality. Yet even in the servantless household, only an ill-organized hostess would have to leave the table to disappear periodically into the kitchen. The perfect hostess would have a battery of hotplates lit by nightlights or heated by electricity on her sideboard. Better still, she might own 'that fashionable adjunct of servantless entertaining', the hostess trolley. A 1970 advertisement for the Ecko Hostess Royale emphasized the consequences of such ownership: 'Buy our … electrically-

Detail from a sectional
elevation of Brighton Pavilion,
showing the proximity of the
kitchen (far right) to the
Banqueting Hall.

Right: An unusually ornate
solution to the problem of
keeping plates warm. The
pedestal once housed a burner.

Below: For 200 years chafing
dishes had been associated
with cooking by ladies. The
chafing dish was said to
liberate diners from spending
'hours at table over tepid food'.

heated trolley and you get a free wife. Free to spend her time
with guests or the family, instead of in the kitchen'.

The hostess trolleys of the 1960s and 1970s may not yet
have the collectable status of their eighteenth-century
forerunners, but they speak of a time when domestic dining
was an event that demanded attention to presentation and
procedures. In our era of 'instant' food and the so-called
'death of the dinner party', a certain poignancy attaches to
these often-ingenious solutions to the problem of how to
keep food warm across the many hours spent at table.

THE ENGLISH AT TABLE: HOGARTH TO GROSSMITH

Left: Hogarth's *A Midnight Modern Conversation*, one of the most celebrated depictions of the English at table. It depicts the after-dinner disorder following too much punch.

Below: The Prince of Wales, languid and replete, surrounded by the remains of his meal, empty bottles and glasses, an overflowing chamber pot, and unpaid food bills.

The habit of dining lends itself particularly to caricature, and has done so since antiquity. In depicting the follies of mankind, authors frequently took the subject of eating and drinking as the vehicle for their satires. Indeed, the most famous satirists of ancient Rome, Horace, Petronius and Juvenal, describe grotesque scenes at ostentatious feasts. If dining together is the time-honoured custom that most signifies and reinforces feelings of hospitality and mutual good will, then to the satirist the table is a good place at which to depict their opposite qualities of selfish vice and folly. This theme recurs in every age. For example, William Langland, the author of the Middle English text *Piers Plowman* (1360–1400), has an amusing but pungent and detailed description of the personified sin of 'Gluttony' drinking and dining to noisome excess in a tavern on a Sunday.

Given this potent mix of ancient custom, the ever-present human desire for the pleasures of the table, and the opportunities for excess, it is no wonder that William Hogarth, that most famous and popular English painter and printmaker, chose to satirize his fellow countrymen at a drinking session. The print entitled *A Midnight Modern Conversation* (1732/3) is perhaps the best-known and most widely pirated image he produced. Appropriately enough, it was copied onto song sheets and ceramic punchbowls and beer mugs (see p.106). Hogarth (who liked a drink himself) shows a group of men, who having dined together earlier, are shown in the ridiculous later stages of intoxication,

Officers 'recruit' their strength by indulging in jellies and sugarplums in the safety of a London confectionery shop.

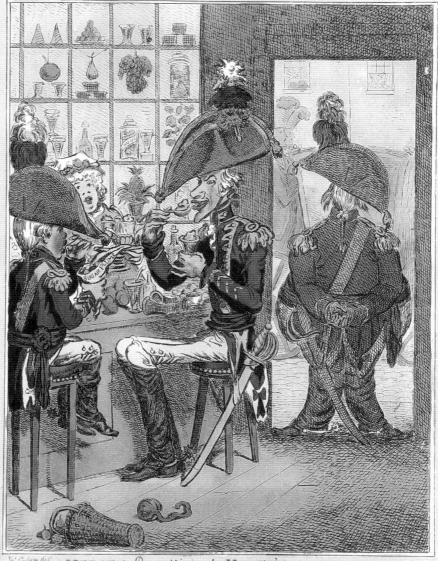

HEROES *Recruiting* at KELSY'S _ vide St James's^t, on the 4th June.

indicating how drink affects even the strongest. The man felled by drink, having lost his wig in the process, is said to be a caricature of James Figg, the prizefighter. The ingredients and the making of the punch, the way of serving it, the proposing of toasts and the drinking of healths, prescribed by custom, have here all too scrupulously been observed by the participants.

No one was safe from the blistering mockery of James Gillray. He had a particular disdain for the vanity of dandified Guard's officers, who, in the eighteenth century, had mostly bought their commissions into fashionable regiments. His *Heroes recruiting at Kelsey's;-or-Guard Day at St James's* (1797), shows a cruel caricature of a certain Captain Birch, in plumed cocked hat, spurs, sabre and jack-boots, devouring a jelly with a spoon from a delicate glass, with more jelly glasses emptied earlier strewn on the counter beside him. The other officer, a mere child, is eating sweets, the legendary sugarplums. Kelsey's was a fruit-shop and a confectioner's in St James's Street, London, near the Court of St James. Gillray is casting doubt on the martial spirit and prowess of these officers, serving in the Royal Guard only by virtue of their influence and purchasing power. His title is a sarcastic pun; the 'Heroes' are 'recruiting' (their strength) in the old sense of restoring themselves by eating, as well as the ostensible meaning of attracting recruits into the army. Showing these soldiers gorging themselves in a sweet shop,

with food more suitable to women and children and other un-warlike civilians, had far more resonance in the manly days of the late eighteenth century. This was before modern advertising was able to portray the eating of sweets as something respectable for grown men.

Gillray recklessly caricatured members of the royal family; one of his fiercest attacks being reserved for the Prince of Wales, later Prince Regent and then George IV. The 'First Gentleman of Europe', once such an elegant figure, steadily became more corpulent, his gourmandizing turning to gluttony. Here, in *A Voluptuary under the Horrors of Digestion* (1792) Gillray portrays him mercilessly; his clothes under tremendous strain, showing he has dined fit to burst. His dazed and uncomfortable expression implies acute indigestion. The remains of a huge meal, complete with

NIGHT.

MORNING.

THE ENGLISH AT TABLE: HOGARTH TO GROSSMITH

decanters of port and brandy (and more empty wine bottles under the circular table), are evidences of his excess. There is a parody of his coat of arms on the candle sconce above, showing a crossed knife and fork with his motto, coronet and feathers. The implication is also that the 'voluptuary' prince has dined greedily alone (or perhaps only with his mistress at the little table), meanly not sharing his table with his family or subjects.

A much lesser known satirist from the silver age of caricature after Gillray's death is 'Shortshanks', a pseudonym for the artist Robert Seymour. His print *Night and Morning* (about 1830) shows the results of dining too well. The first scene depicts a bon viveur, with a drinker's reddened nose, at the final course of the meal, with the nuts and peaches being washed down with copious glasses of the dessert port and sherry. The morning scene shows the dreadful results of dining and drinking too much, with the twin demons of a hangover and acute indigestion attacking their victim. Nuts at the end of the meal were the fashion then, hence the expression 'from soup to nuts' meaning from the first to the last courses (i.e. the whole meal), and by extension, meaning 'from the beginning to the end' of anything.

One result of the Napoleonic wars was that a substantial number of prisoners of war were held captive in Britain. One of these had his revenge as the anonymous artist of satirical prints published in Paris in 1814. Signing himself '*un français prisonnier de Guerre*' he depicted in ruthless detail the peculiar and brutish habits of the English in a set of '*scènes anglaises dessinées à Londres*'. This print entitled *L'après-*

dinée des Anglais shows the last stage of a meal, which has degenerated into a drinking bout around the punch bowl. Although it is often held that the tablecloth was normally removed for the dessert in nineteenth-century Britain, the artist has shown it still on the table, and it is likely customs varied according to time and situation. The removal of the cloth was usually the signal for drinking to begin in earnest. Yet the detail of the chamber pot taken from a cupboard in the sideboard, after the ladies had withdrawn from the dining room, was indeed normal practice. To add insult to injury, the picture on the dining room wall shows an English landscape with heavy rain as the main feature.

George and Walter Weedon Grossmith are famous as the authors of *The Diary of a Nobody*, a gentle satire at the expense of Mr Pooter, the archetypal member of the lower middle classes. It was serialized in *Punch* in 1888 and reprinted as a book in 1892. Weedon's drawing of Mr Burwin-Fosselton at supper is a portrait of an aspiring actor (as yet only a member of the 'Holloway Comedians') demonstrating his ability to imitate Henry Irving. His lack of manners at table distressed Mr Pooter, who had mistakenly had the kindness to invite him to supper. Mr Pooter noted that the actor 'sank so low down in his chair that his chin was almost on a level with the table, and twice he kicked Carrie under the table, upset his wine, and flashed a knife uncomfortably near Gowing's face.' This mildly satiric portrait has come a long way from the unsparing savagery of Gillray, yet the theme of the dining table as suitable place to mock the follies of mankind still survives.

Opposite top: The brutish after-dinner customs of the English, as witnessed by a French prisoner of war.

Opposite bottom: One of many satires showing the evil consequence of over-indulgence in food or drink. Dining is rarely depicted in English art, satires excepted.

Right: Illustration to *The Diary of a Nobody*. The dining habits of the Victorian lower-middle classes were a subject of humour.

LUXURY GLASS FOR WINE AND BEER, 1550–1720

It is a world to see in these our days, wherein gold and silver most aboundeth … our gentility, as loathing those metals [because of the plenty] do now generally choose rather the Venice glasses, both for our wine and beer … And as this is seen in the gentility, so in the wealthy communality the like desire of glass is not neglected.

WILLIAM HARRISON, *DESCRIPTION OF ENGLAND*, 1586

Indeed, glass is the ideal material for serving drinks. Its transparency allows the examination of the colour and clarity of its contents; yet it is light and easy to clean and does not retain odours or taints. Wealthy Romans used glass vessels for drinking and decanting as well as for storing liquids, while during the Middle Ages this precious material continued to be enjoyed, if only at the highest levels of society.

Harrison's admired Venetian glass came from the island of Murano, where a highly organized luxury glass industry had developed by the late twelfth century. Backed by a vast trading fleet and connected to overland trade routes, Murano enjoyed an unparalleled period of expansion from the late fifteenth century. Venetian glasses found their way across Europe – not only to the tables of powerful courts,

but also to the grand houses of the nobility and rich merchants as well, as Harrison testifies. International demand in the sixteenth and the seventeenth centuries drew many Venetian glassmakers to leave Murano and set up new glass-houses in other European cities, where they produced drinking glasses in the Venetian manner, known as '*à la façon de Venise*'.

Because of the extreme fragility of the material, and the uses to which they were put, few drinking glasses have survived intact. Very little is known about drinking glasses of the medieval period, but the variety of shapes and types seems to have increased significantly during the sixteenth and seventeenth centuries.

Harrison's book also describes the English custom of calling for a drink from the cupboard (sideboard), and the manner in which the glasses were shared:

As for drink, it is usually filled in pots, goblets, jugs, bowls of silver in noblemen's houses; also in fine Venice glasses of all forms: all of which notwithstanding are seldom set on the table, but each one, as necessity urgeth, calleth for a cup of such drink as him listeth to have, so that, when he has tasted

Opposite: A clear glass is used for red wine and a green *roemer* for white. The *roemer* is mounted in a silver-gilt *bekerschroef* to enhance its status.

Right: The guests drink red wine from tall-stemmed shallow glasses, displaying the Italian courtiers' *'sprezzatura'* – the art of making 'whatever is done appear without effort'.

A design for an elaborate trick glass of 1617 that mixed water with wine as it was being drunk.

of it, he delivereth the cup again to some one of the standers by, who making it clean by pouring out the drink that remaineth, restoreth it to the cupboard from whence he fetched the same. By this device ... some tippling is furthermore cut off.

Two or more people often shared a single glass in this way, as can be seen in many paintings of elegant gatherings. In Paolo Veronese's *Wedding at Cana*, where the biblical event is shown in a contemporary courtly context, few glasses are set on the table, while refilling takes place on the floor in the foreground.

Each society had its preferred type of drinking vessel. Veronese's painting shows a typical Italian form, the so-called '*tazza*', the use of which spread with the fashion for

LUXURY GLASS FOR WINE AND BEER, 1550–1720

Left: 'In Vino Veritas': inscription on the 'dragon-stemmed' goblet. The green glass *roemer* was popular in Germany and the Netherlands for white wine.

Opposite top: Communal and individual glasses for drinking beer. The German towns, in particular, had a strong tradition of drinking vessels that were passed round the table.

Opposite below: Two English glasses of about 1700–20, made before the great proliferation of specialized English glass types.

Venetian glass. This is a shallow dish on a high foot for drinking red wine; it was extremely difficult to drink from without spillage, an act only achieved by those with the most sophisticated manners. Goblets with a deeper bowl were supplied for less splendid or less formal occasions. In Central Europe – where the custom of communal drinking required large glasses for passing around the table from guest to guest – tall cylindrical '*Stangengläser*' and '*Humpen*' were used for beer.

It was probably during the sixteenth century that specialized types of drinking glasses for different drinks became customary, different types appearing for wine, beer and spirits. In 1562 Johann Mathesius, a German priest, noted:

It is true that a red wine looks truly beautiful in a white and clear Venetian glass, and gives off its shine and light, when the glass would stand in the sun or in front of a light by night. As also a pale wine gives its colours like a rainbow through a green glass, because the reflection increases through wine and water.

This usage is confirmed by seventeenth-century Dutch still-life paintings, which show a remarkable variety of goblets in the Venetian style and almost invariably filled with red wine; among them are tall flute glasses, a characteristically Dutch shape. The optical challenge of depicting the reflections in green glass '*roemers*', another Dutch type for drinking white wine, seemed to have delighted many of the greatest still life painters. The 'prunts' (or bosses) on the lower part of these *roemers* developed from a medieval tradition: in addition to being decorative they served the practical function of providing a grip for greasy hands, which was essential at a time when forks were not yet commonly used. Beakers of various forms are usually shown filled with beer, recognizable from the layer of foam on top of the liquid.

The pen and ink drawing illustrated here is from an extraordinary collection of designs, by several artists, specially made for members of the Medici family of Florence. The seventeenth-century examples provide a glimpse of some of the most elaborate drinking vessels ever made. This example, by Jacopo Ligozzi, shows a *tazza* in which water could be mixed with red wine while its contents were being drunk. In the margins Ligozzi added detailed instructions for its manufacture and use. Although it is now difficult to believe that such sophisticated follies were ever produced, fragments of similar objects survive in the Medici collections. Such glasses were intended to impress and

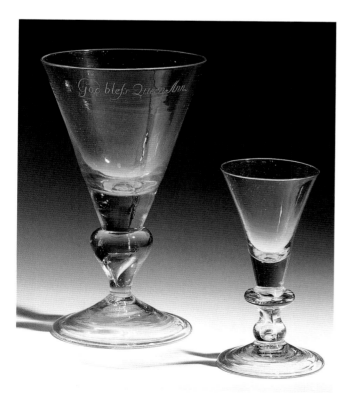

entertain guests at special occasions and were probably never expected to last. Certainly, we know from sixteenth-century accounts that the finest fragile Murano glasses could be smashed as an expression of great joy at an important wedding feast.

During the third quarter of the seventeenth century glassmakers all across Europe sought to make stronger, heavier and more robust glasses. One of the main reasons for this was the increasing popularity of engraving techniques, which required thicker-walled vessels; and glassmakers were inspired to imitate the qualities of the costly mineral rock-crystal, which was often decorated in this way. In 1670s England this prompted the development and patenting of a new type of lead-rich glass. Heavier, clearer and more lustrous than any glass made before, the new lead-glass was suitable for simplified, robust types of drinking vessels, which in England were mostly left undecorated. Its worldwide success came in the following century, when overall cut and polished decoration fully exploited its refractive qualities. Cut-glass chandeliers sparkled light around the rooms, while on the dinner tables below the light of candles was reflected in the thousands of cut-glass facets decorating goblets and decanters, which were now made in increasing quantities, sorts and sizes.

SERVING SWEETMEATS

The banquet was 12 vast chargers pild up so high, as those who sat one against another could hardly see one another, of these sweetmeates which doubtless were some dayes piling up in that exquisite manner, the [Venetian] Ambassadors touched not, but leaving them to the spectators who came in curiosity to see the dinner.

JOHN EVELYN, DESCRIBING A BANQUET HELD BY CHARLES II IN 1685

The term 'sweetmeats' indicates the broad category of sugared and spiced fruits, conserves, creams, biscuits, jellies and other confectionery that made up the final 'sweet' course of a grand 'entertainment'. They were highly decorative and often coloured with natural dyes such as saffron, powder of violets, spinach juice or cochineal, and some were even embellished with gold leaf. They were also costly, as their essential ingredients – the spices and sugars – had to be imported and specially prepared, and as their manufacture was often laborious. There were two types of sweetmeats – wet and dry – and their consistency and the way in which they were eaten dictated the way they were served. The service of sweetmeats, and the fruit that often accompanied them, constituted the most splendid and fanciful part of a meal, as the elaboration of the display of these foodstuffs was heightened in accordance with their extravagance and cost. Their extent and the manner of their service gave a measure of a host's esteem for his guests, and the presentation was the benchmark by which the occasion was finally judged.

In the sixteenth and early seventeenth centuries this final course was served as a separate meal known as a 'banquet'. This usually took place in a room other than the dining hall, which was cleared or 'voided' for dancing or promenading. Alternatively, it might be taken out of doors; or, as in court

Bottom left: One from a set of bowls for an Elizabethan 'banquet' – a separate meal of suckets, marchpane, comfits, sweetened creams, or other sweetmeats.

Right: Food for thought: the delicacies are seductive, but the moral is that Christian charity is preferable to indulgence.

Below right: The piercing of the dish echoes the patterns of 'Kraak' porcelain; such dishes were probably for dry sweetmeats.

circles, the participants might adjourn to a separate banqueting house. Here sweetmeats, such as spiced wafers, biscuits and comfits, would be displayed on tables following thematic layouts given in culinary manuals, and served in silver-gilt spice bowls, standing cups or dishes of Chinese porcelain (still a luxury at this time), accompanied by spiced or sweet wines such as hypocras and muscadine. The engraved spice bowl shown here is from a set of six, a luxury for an intimate gathering. We know from household inventories that gilded sets for sweetmeats were popular, but few survive today. The highly detailed central engraved scenes would not have been revealed until the bowl had been emptied – surprising and entertaining the guests – indicating that the bowls were intended for use rather than reserved for display on a buffet. Osias Beert's still life of the early seventeenth-century shows a standing silver cup of a type

used for both wine and dry sweetmeats during these years. Some dry sweetmeats, such as marchpanes, iced biscuits and sugar confections, formed decorative centrepieces themselves, supporting other sweetmeats and fruit.

The vessels in which sweetmeats were served contributed greatly to the splendour of the display. Silver vessels, flatware and even pewter for the sweetmeats and fruit were gilded (in part to hinder tarnishing), which set them apart from the other plate and reinforced the special status of the course. Glass and porcelain were also widely used, particularly from the late seventeenth century. Indeed, many found them more suitable than silver for delicacies, as they were hygienic and did not taint the flavour of the sweets; and the painted patterns and clear white surfaces of porcelain provided a wonderful background for decorative food. François Massialot in his *Nouvelles instructions pour les confitures* (1692) insisted on

SERVING
SWEETMEATS

The bowl of the Venetian glass is so shallow that it can hardly have been intended for wine, but, like the '*Schwartzlot*'-painted Bohemian glass, was probably for sweetmeats.

'*China*' for serving wet sweetmeats, and Robert May, in his *Accomplisht Cook* (1678) recommended 'little round jelly glasses' for creams, stacked upon gilded salvers. Silver, glass and porcelain utensils for banqueting or the dessert could also be brought out for christenings, funerals and other gatherings where a full dinner was not provided.

Beginning in the seventeenth century, the 'banquet' ceased to be served as a separate meal and evolved into what we know today as the dessert, a term that derives from the French *desservir*, meaning to clear the table, and one that recalls the Elizabethan 'void'. (The term 'banquet', on the other hand, eventually came to be reserved for a sumptuous meal of both sweet and savoury foods). Although incorporated into the main meal, the service of sweetmeats was no less elaborate than in earlier years. The eighteenth century saw the widespread adoption of epergnes (see p.66), tiered ceramic centrepieces (often cast with real shells), and porcelain figurines bearing scallops for serving sweetmeats at table; alternatively they could be offered in

ceramic trays and compartment dishes similar to those for pickles, or in glass cups. Garden layouts and amorous themes became popular embellishments for the dessert course: sweetmeats were set out in bowls among *parterres* of coloured sands and silk, with marzipan and sugar hedges and sugar-paste or porcelain figures or beasts. By the middle of the century *parterres* and table ornaments were often placed on plateaux of mirrored glass, which reflected not only the display of the dessert but also the lighting and decoration of the room (see p.92).

Wet sweetmeats such as syllabubs, creams, custards, trifles and jellies tended to be frothy or quite liquid and needed to be contained. They were either served in small bell-shaped vessels of porcelain or glass, or they were set in decoratively shaped moulds, and then turned out and presented on dishes. The froth resembling whipped cream that sits on top of the glasses depicted in Philippe Mercier's painting is probably 'Whip't' syllabub, and the tapering shape of the glasses supports the syllabub, preventing it from sinking.

Such glasses were served on salvers of silver, as shown by Mercier, or glass. The latter can be seen in two satirical prints by Gillray (see pp.72–3). One of these includes a set of salvers loaded with glasses and stacked to form a pyramid (as was common practice, to judge from prints and eighteenth-century glass cutters' trade cards); and the other shows a confectioner proffering 'jellies' from a tall-stemmed salver, which she holds over a counter strewn with empty jelly glasses.

Wet sweetmeats served in individual glasses or porcelain cups would be eaten with spoons, as in the second Gillray print, and most dry sweetmeats were eaten with the fingers. However, berries, candied citrus fruits or ginger preserved in syrup would stain the fingers and were often eaten with a fork. Fruits preserved in syrup were known as 'wet suckets' in the sixteenth century, and the earliest forks are therefore known as 'sucket forks'. These are listed in inventories of Charles V and Charles VI, and Henry VIII's inventory lists table sculpture hung with 12 fancy knives and forks for

banqueting. The introduction of the sucket fork as a luxury exclusively for piercing and conveying sweetmeats to the mouth revolutionized table manners, as it led not only to the development of the dessert fork, but more importantly to the modern table fork, which few in the West could do without today.

Above: Mercier shows a salver set with jelly or 'Whip't syllabub' glasses and a covered sweetmeat glass. Note the manner of pouring wine.

Right: The 'sucket' fork of the 16th century was a mannerist creation quite unlike the utilitarian table fork of the late 17th century.

Ice-Cream

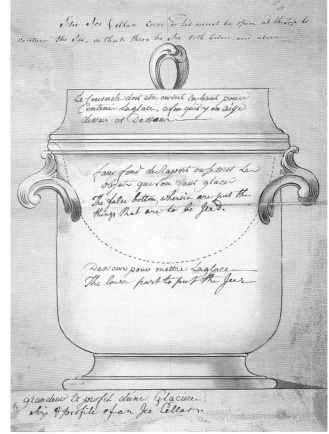

Above: Before the invention of the refrigerator ice for drinks and ice-cream was stored underground throughout the year.

Right: A drawing of a French ice-cream pail from the Leeds pottery pattern books. Piracy of design was rife in the 18th-century ceramic trade.

The popular perception that ice-cream, along with the Renaissance, the opera, the Ferrari, the Lambretta, the Venetian blind and every variety of pasta, must rank as one of Italy's supreme contributions to western culture, would not be far from the truth. It was, in fact, the Roman custom of using snow to add to wine and to chill food that was revived by the new wealthy and cultured classes of sixteenth-century Italy, where underground 'snow-pits' with thatched roofs were first devised in order to store compacted snow and ice throughout the summer. After these tentative beginnings, cultural ties between Italy and France extended the fashion for using ice to Paris, and thus eventually to the rest of Europe.

Italian cooks continued to develop recipes for semi-frozen desserts during the seventeenth century, despite a widespread belief that ice was bad for the health. In France, much ingenuity was applied to the preparation of these ices as the *pièces de résistance* of lavish dinners given at the court of Louis XIV. The first royal ice-house was built at Versailles in 1664, followed in 1670 by the opening of the first ice-cream shop in Paris, and in 1692 by two cookery books that included full instructions for making ice-cream at a domestic level. It was in France that the exiled Charles II and his followers developed a taste not only for tea, coffee and chocolate, but also for frozen desserts. Still as yet an unseasonable delicacy affordable only by the Court, the Sovereign's Table at the feast of St George at Windsor in May 1671 included but a single 'Plate of Ice Cream'.

Led by the French, the eighteenth century witnessed a flowering in the arts of cooking and dining. For eating frozen food, a small cup with a handle was soon devised. Glass, which was cheap, imitated the appearance of ice and also showed its highly coloured contents to best advantage, remains to this day the favourite material. For more formal dining, Chinese porcelain 'custard cups' – of which 100,000 were imported into London between 1699 and 1705 – may have been used; these would probably have served ices on smarter tables until the development of porcelain-making in Europe offered possibilities for new shapes. If the '24 White Cups with two handles for Ice Cream' of Meissen porcelain presented to Sir Charles Hanbury Williams in 1748 were probably similar to Chinese prototypes, by about 1760 the new prestigious Sèvres factory of Louis XV had designed an entire range of porcelain tablewares for ice-cream. The *équipage*, which sometimes included matching silver-gilt ice 'trowels' (see p.56), consisted of the *seau à glace* with its inner liner surrounded on all sides by ice, the single-handled *tasse à glace*, and the special footed serving trays, the *plateau Bouret* and *soucoupe à pied*, to hold six or seven *tasses*. The ice-pails were reproduced in *faience*, and provided models for accurate copies made by other continental porcelain factories, as well as for ambitious English makers. The ice-cream cups of many English manufacturers, however, tended to follow the more adaptable lidded two-handled Sèvres *pot à jus*.

From the sixteenth century, until the invention of the first commercial electric 'Frigidaire' in the USA in 1915, the manufacture of ice-cream depended on natural ice. Into a bucket of ice, with salt or saltpetre added to enhance its freezing properties, would be plunged a watertight container filled with the prepared mixture to be frozen. This would intermittently be turned and agitated to quicken the freezing action, while the container would be opened periodically so that the ice forming on the inside could be scraped away with a spatula. Two pints of ice-cream could be produced in this way in about 40 minutes, and apart from the addition of a hand-cranking mechanism towards the middle of the nineteenth century, the method continued unchanged until

the First World War. The containers, known from their French derivation as *sabbatiers, salbotières, sarbotières* or *sorbetières*, were at first constructed of tin-plate. By the mid-eighteenth century, however, sabbatiers and moulds of heavy pewter – which were resistant to salt corrosion and could incorporate tight-fitting hinged lids – were exclusively recommended by influential cookery writers.

From the beginning, two distinct types of ice were favoured: frozen fruit pulp or *glace rare,* and the firmer *fromage glacé* made with cream. The former confectioner to Queen Anne, Mrs Mary Eales, published the first English ice-cream recipes in 1718, after which the fashion spread rapidly to the middle classes, to cafés, and to confectioners who supplied ices as part of their catering activities. By 1765, half of Hannah Glasse's dessert recipes were for ice, which she declared 'is a thing used in all desserts, as it is to be had both winter and summer, and … always to be had at the confectioners'.

Sèvres porcelain for ice-cream and chilled wine set out at Waddesdon Manor (the bottle is modern).

ICE-CREAM

Towards the middle of the eighteenth century dessert tables of the wealthy might be laid with *trompe l'oeil* ices, some made in individual moulds but all cleverly painted and embellished in the guise of fish, meat or vegetables. Exotic flavours such as pistachio, chocolate, white coffee and even brown bread were also introduced at this period, and increasingly ices were made in shaped pewter moulds, to be turned out onto plates like jellies. The pyramids of glass salvers loaded with filled jelly and syllabub glasses, shown in so many prints of the period, would have been quite unsuitable for melting ice-cream.

If the English needed further encouragement to appreciate ices, this was amply provided by the cafés of Paris during the occupation in 1815. In London, confectioners such as Gunters of the Strand relied on ice imported from Iceland to satisfy their customers, a situation that improved towards the mid-nineteenth century with regular shipments from Norway. For wealthy households, a Derby porcelain dinner service might include ice-pails and cups copied from Sèvres, while more modest bone-china versions made by Spode and Davenport were available; cheaper still were versions made in creamware. The grand and richly decorated 'Warwick' and dolphin-supported pails made by Chamberlain were clearly intended to double as ornamental vases for the sideboard, and with the gradual introduction towards the middle of the nineteenth-century of service *à la russe* (in which dishes were served by waiters to guests at the table), these ice-pails became obsolescent. Henceforward, individual ice glasses, mainly cut-glass and made throughout the century in the latest styles, would be served with wafers in the home, just as in the ice-cream cafés of so many European cities.

From this period ice-cream also began increasingly to form an important part of life at a popular level. Regular shipments of ice harvested in Iceland and Norway supplied the needs of commercial and domestic ice-cream making; flavours became standardized, with vanilla a clear favourite from about 1850; the new railways enabled seaside towns to open up to the masses escaping the smoky confines of industrialized cities; scoops began to be served on cheap pressed-glass 'licks' that needed no spoon; Italian immigrants poured into other European countries and the USA to make and sell ices on the street; and in the 1860s the first experimental (and highly explosive) freezing machines were made using the same principle of compression and evaporation still employed by refrigerators today. By 1900 ices were no longer a novelty, merely a necessity of life. Ice-cream truly belonged to the masses.

The ice-cream pail (or *seau à glace*) from the Duke of Wellington's 'Egyptian Service'.

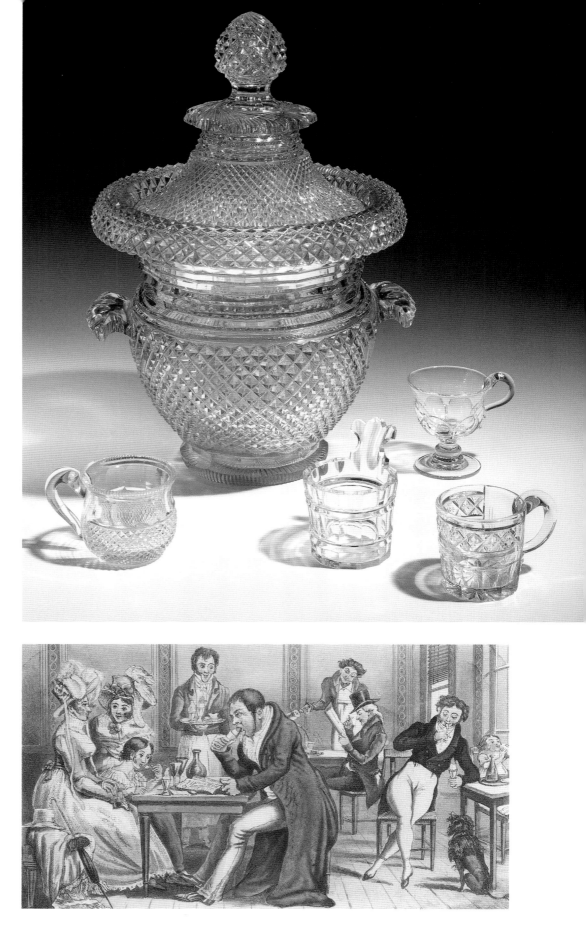

A massively-thick cut-glass ice-cream pail of about 1810, together with a selection of 'piggins' and other cups for serving ice-cream.

John Bull and his family shown eating ice-cream from conical glasses at a London 'ice café' around 1820.

PORCELAIN FOR THE DESSERT

Above: A plate from Meissen's celebrated Swan Service (intended for both dinner and dessert), flanked by two dessert plates, that on the right made for Catherine the Great.

Left: The French porcelain factories introduced several new vessels for serving the dessert, including small tureens for ground sugar and ice-cream pails.

Chinese porcelain – familiar in Europe by the sixteenth century – was technically superior to any ceramic material made in the West before about 1700, and European potters made strenuous attempts to imitate it. Meissen, around 1710, became the first to succeed, opening the way for a succession of Continental factories owned by noble families and run as a matter of competitive prestige. Often made as diplomatic gifts, their luxury wares could be very costly indeed.

Technical problems in firing large wares delayed the introduction of extensive services with matching decoration (made at Meissen by 1729). Of course, potters had long repeated standard patterns, and made sets of wares, but the matching service was something new, reflecting a shift in dining etiquette. From about the same date polite society increasingly required wares that served specific functions only – in contrast to the multi-purpose bowls and dishes of previous centuries – and required also that wherever possible these should be for individual use. These changes had a revolutionary impact on ceramic production, and resulted in services that were often elaborate in their decoration and large and complex in their make-up as well.

Great ingenuity went into making ceramics for the dessert, the climax of the meal. Like the fruit and confectionery of the dessert it was made to serve, fine porcelain was costly and fragile, and it satisfied the same taste for artifice and luxury. And being hygienic and odour-free, it was favoured above metals, which were not always thought 'conformable' to the 'present *whim* of taste'. Curiously, however, the same

By virtue of its size and decoration this dessert service was the most expensive that had been made at Sèvres up to 1766.

plates could be used for sweet and savoury courses, even in some of the grandest services, long after Meissen's introduction of special pierced dessert plates in the year 1742.

Meissen set the fashions followed in the first half of the eighteenth century, after which the royal French factory at Sèvres took the lead. Among the new object types introduced by the French factories at Vincennes-Sèvres and Chantilly were shaped dishes for the dessert and special vessels for cooling drinks and serving ice-cream, many of which can be seen in the part-service shown here.

A service such as this would clearly only have been bought by the very wealthy (and it was in fact one of the most expensive made at Sèvres by the mid-1760s), and would have been used as to make a statement about taste, wealth and political might. Meissen's Swan Service, for example, was made for the most powerful minister in Saxony and Poland; it comprised 2,200 pieces and served 206. Similarly, the Sèvres plate shown here is from a 797-piece service, costing an exceptional 360,000 *livres*, made for Catherine the Great.

No services of comparable richness were made in eighteenth-century England, and although some factories attempted to make luxury wares, most concentrated on less wealthy markets. The Derby dessert plate painted with grapes, for example, is from a 44-piece service sold to a Cheshire landowner for only £33. In 1787 the Derby management hoped to sell exports to France, but found there would be little demand for 'common' English porcelain, as 'there are but two Sorts of people in France, one rich & the other poor', and the English porcelains would meet the needs of neither.

Partly because England lacked an aristocracy on the Continental model, and partly because of technical problems, large richly decorated English services are rare until the early nineteenth century, when the Worcester and Derby factories specialized in them. By the late nineteenth century the market for porcelain had expanded greatly, and modestly priced dessert wares were available through such large wholesalers as Silber and Fleming, whose trade catalogues illustrated every type of domestic good.

SCULPTURE FOR THE DESSERT, 1680–1910

Although ephemeral, sugar paste figures could be by the best court artists, as with these allegorical groups attributed to Cirro Ferri.

An elaborate dessert setting with confectionery parterre, sweetmeat glasses, and figures set out on a mirror plateau.

It probably comes as a surprise to many that the porcelain figures we are familiar with today had their origins in table decorations in wax and sugar paste. These had been made from medieval times for royal wedding feasts, and Germany, in particular, had a strong tradition of creating elaborate tableaux in which confectionery figures were combined with architectural features in landscape settings.

A vivid impression of the type of symbolism favoured for the grandest of table settings can be gleaned from the following account of a royal marriage of 1738. Devised by a Saxon court confectioner, the first evening's tableau 'represented Love and Constancy, and alluded throughout in all the figures to the present marriage of her Majesty'. In the middle of the table was a temple, 'the cupola of blue sugar', at the entrance to which stood the god of marriage, and on either side of it were two intertwined hearts 'properly marked out on a narrow band of glass, decked with red confectionery'.

Amorous themes were especially popular at Meissen, the factory that took the crucial step of making figures for the table in porcelain.

Originally intended as expressions of dynastic power and to celebrate marriages and political allegiances, by the sixteenth century allegorical themes had been introduced into these ensembles, and by the seventeenth century many were largely decorative and above all intended to entertain 'and gratifie the Eye'. Although ephemeral, the finest work demanded great skill, and some sugar paste sculptures were by the best court artists: those in Lenardi's engraving, for example, are probably by the Roman painter, sculptor and designer Cirro Ferri. These were described as modelled 'to the utmost skill of a Statuary' and were 'afterwards, sent as Presents to the Greatest Ladies'. Later, less elaborate pieces might be broken open to reveal verses before being eaten, as James Boswell witnessed in Berlin in 1762. The 'proper arrangement' of such allegorical figures, made to accompany grand desserts, required considerable knowledge of history, poetry, mythology, architecture and perspective, according to a German housekeepers' manual of 1785.

Meissen was the first factory to make table decorations in the more durable (and reusable) material of porcelain. These were produced from the 1730s, when the factory was in the hands of Count Brühl, the most powerful man in Saxony and Poland. Count Brühl entertained on a magnificent scale, and commissioned the celebrated Swan Service (devised in part by a confectioner), which sat as many as 206 'at one table'. This, and his extravagant table decorations, greatly impressed one Englishman, who revelled in its theatre in 1748:

When the dessert was set on, I thought it was the most wonderful thing I ever beheld. I fancyd myself either in a Garden or at the Opera, But I [could] not imagine that I was at Dinner. In the middle of the Table was the Fountain ... at least eight foot high, which ran all the while with Rose-water, and tis said that this Piece alone cost six thousand Dollars.

Architectural ensembles on this scale would have been vastly expensive one-off productions, but Meissen's sets of small figures were made in great quantity and were widely copied elsewhere; like Meissen, many of these other factories made figures that also served as sweetmeat stands. The royal

SCULPTURE FOR THE DESSERT, 1680–1910

French factory at Sèvres, however, initially experienced great difficulties in firing glazed figures, and spurred on by necessity created an entirely new ceramic genre – the biscuit (unglazed) figure. Although porous and easily stained, this new material was much used for table decorations (examples can be seen set out for a dessert on pages 80–81). Introduced in 1751, biscuit porcelain was in due course imitated elsewhere, notably at the Derby factory, which, in 1773, advertised biscuit figures as being 'particularly suited for the Embellishment of Desserts'.

By this date the fashion for porcelain table settings in Britain was more than 20 years old. In 1753 Horace Walpole had noted that:

Jellies, biscuits, sugar plumbs and creams have long since given way to harlequins, gondoliers, Turks, Chinese and shepherdesses of Saxon [Meissen] china. But these, unconnected, and only seeming to wander among groves of curled paper and silk flowers, were soon discovered to be too insipid and unmeaning. By degrees … cottages rose in sugar, and temples in barley-sugar; pigmy Neptunes in cars of cockle-shells triumphed over oceans of looking glass or seas of silver tissue … Confectioners found their trade moulder away, while toy-men and china-shops were the only fashionable purveyors of the last stage of polite entertainments.

Parson Woodforde admired a small landscape table centrepiece of this type when he dined with the Bishop of Norwich in 1783, indicating that they were not confined to the fashionable metropolitan world.

Despite Walpole's comment that the confectioner's trade had 'mouldered away', sugar and wax were never entirely superseded by porcelain, even for figures, and still less for architectural elements (which were often made of glass). Rather, a variety of materials could be used in combination, as is clear from the following passage from the housekeepers' manual of 1785:

The easiest representations at great desserts are pleasure-gardens, with promenades, buildings, fountains, *parterres*, vases and statues, of which the last porcelain factories make

One of 125 architectural fantasies designed by the great French chef Antonin Carême and intended to be realized in confectionery; Carême held that cooking was an architectural art.

the prettiest … thus saving the confectioner much work, since previously he was obliged to make such vases and figures of tragacanth paste or caramel-sugar. Nevertheless, the confectioner often introduces tragacanth-work amongst the porcelain, if he cannot procure [items] in porcelain … Similarly, he frequently introduces figures … modelled in wax … The centre-piece of a table-decoration is likely to be of mirror-plate or merely clear glass, and the architectural ornaments are also of glass.

Mirror plateaux of the type mentioned in these quotations were very fashionable in the mid-eighteenth century, when they were often set out with elaborate parterre (formal garden patterns) made out of mousseline, marzipan or pasteboard filled with coloured sugar or sand. The engraving here from *Le Cannameliste Français* (1751, written by Joseph Gilliers – confectioner to the deposed King of Poland), shows a mirror plateaux set out with sweetmeat glasses, parterre and porcelain figures. Plateaux continued to be used well into the nineteenth-century; one used by the Prince of Wales in 1811 ran the whole length of tables set for 2,000 people. However, they did not long survive the mid-nineteenth century's adoption of service *à la russe* and the growing preference for floral table decorations.

By the early nineteenth century porcelain figures had largely fallen from use at the dessert, but they were occasionally revived for state occasions: the Berlin porcelain figures illustrated here were first made for royal wedding celebrations in 1905. Work in sugar and wax likewise fell from fashion after about 1800, although confectionery centrepieces continued to be made for state dinners – as with the architectural confections designed by the great French chef Antonin Carême – and this decorative tradition survives in the wedding cakes made today. Writing in the 1820s, the London confectioner Guglielmo Jarrin regretted that modelling in sugar paste had given way to pastry chefs' work. Modelling in sugar, he argued, required 'dexterity, much patience, some knowledge of mythology, of history, and of the arts of modelling and design', qualifications, he lamented, that were 'seldom possessed by the mere pastry-cook'.

Centrepieces in the 18th and 19th centuries could be on a scale almost inconceivable today. This detail is of a surtout 6.641 m (21³/4 ft) long.

Below: A late example of a porcelain sculptural table ensemble: a set first made for the wedding of a German crown prince in 1905.

Serving and Cooling Wine

Put clean and fresh water into the tubbes ... the one to keep the drink fresh, the other to refresh the glasses and cuppes, to the end that we may drink fresh, for it is very hot.
PIERRE ERRONDELLE, *THE FRENCH GARDEN*, 1605

Left: The Macclesfield fountain, cistern and cooler of 1719 – weighing nearly 2239 oz – comprise the only complete set still intact.

Opposite: At this French dinner each guest has a wine cooler. No glasses are laid on the table and servants offer water to dilute wine to taste.

Wine has been a key element of dining from antiquity to the present, and the articles to cool and serve it amongst the grandest in the dining room. From the medieval period to around 1700 vessels for wine were displayed on the buffet to create the greatest theatrical effect. By the eighteenth century its service had become an elaborate and ceremonial process, demanding a variety of equipment – from wine coolers and monteiths to coasters, corkscrews and bottle tickets.

Until the mid-twelfth century most wines drunk in Britain were British, but the marriage of Henry II and Eleanor of Aquitaine in 1152 opened up the market for French wines, which soon became ubiquitous. By the mid-eighteenth century, port and sherry were also popular, port having found favour during the wars with France, when Portuguese wines enjoyed low import duties. With the renewal of trade with France in the 1770s, availability of sparkling champagne

(as opposed to the flat variety drunk previously) was one benefit. Sir Robert Walpole's wine account for Houghton Hall is an interesting snapshot of aristocratic consumption in 1730. He bought '2400 bottles of White Lisbon (white port), 650 of Canary Sack, 1300 of Red Port, 4010 bottles of Claret, 200 of Champaign and 390 of Burgundy' from his wine merchant, at a total cost of £1,302. Wine could be drunk at any meal, even breakfast, as recorded by Queen Charlotte when visiting Cotehele in 1789: 'at breakfast ... we eat off the Old Family Pewter and used Silver knives, Forks and Spoons ... the Decanters are of the year 1646 the names of the Wines burnt in the Earthenware'. The importance of wine at dinner was reinforced by the decoration of dining rooms and plate, which very often incorporated references to Bacchus, the god of wine.

Wine was generally drunk chilled, irrespective of its colour, which required a ready supply of ice supplied by a thriving trade with the Baltic ports. In wealthier households ice was accumulated in ponds during winter and stored in subterranean ice-houses. Until the late seventeenth century, wine was held in barrels in the cellar and brought up in bottles or decanters. It was not until corks were introduced that wine was aged in the bottle, which took on the cylindrical shape familiar today, as this could be stacked in cellars. Wine required cooling before it could be served, and this led to the introduction of a number of vessels in which it could stand in crushed ice.

Equipment for serving wine obviously reflected the way in which the meal was served. During the seventeenth century, for example, glasses and bottles were not set on the table. A diner who wished to drink summoned a servant, who filled a glass from bottles cooling on the sideboard and presented it on a small, footed salver. The glass was drained immediately and returned so that it could be rinsed and refilled. It was therefore necessary to have the equivalent of the modern day dishwasher and refrigerator to hand; and in the grandest households a fountain, cistern and cooler would be set up — sometimes in a specially designed alcove – to one side in the dining room. Water was drawn from the fountain to rinse glasses in the cistern, and these would then be filled from the bottles in the wine cooler below. If made of silver, the ensemble would be one of the most expensive purchases a nobleman could make. The set ordered by Thomas Parker, 1st Earl of Macclesfield, in 1719–20 cost a staggering £1,220 (compared to £60–£120 for a coach).

By the mid-eighteenth century, service *à la française* was

SERVING AND COOLING WINE

well established in Britain, and the focus of attention had moved from the buffet to the dining table itself. The single bottle cooler, or ice pail, was introduced as a result. This was either placed on the table, or, on less formal occasions, on the floor behind a diner's chair, and servants still brought fresh glasses on salvers, and replaced empty bottles. Another refinement particularly popular in France was an individual serving table – with a recess for a wine cooler, space for a glass cooler, and a shelf beneath for plates – which stood within reach of each guest. At the end of the meal, the cloth was cleared, the dessert was laid out and wines were placed on the table. After one or two glasses, the ladies withdrew to make tea, and the men stayed to enjoy the wine in a more relaxed fashion, sometimes for considerable periods of time. This created a need for coasters, or bottle 'slides', which prevented damage to the table. Initially for single bottles, and with low sides, coasters became ever more elaborate, developing into rolling chariots for two bottles, or conceits such as the jolly boats illustrated here. A number of different wines could be served with dessert, so several wagons or 'slides' might be required.

Glass and silver decanters provided an alternative to bottles. They first appeared in the late seventeenth century, and were well established by 1750. However served at the table, drinks required identification, and so the 'bottle ticket' or wine label was introduced. Hung round the bottle or decanter's neck, these were usually made of silver or enamelled copper, and were inscribed with generic names. Some had highly fanciful designs – bats with outstretched wings, for example – and they were often supplied in sets. Bottle tickets gradually fell from use during the nineteenth century, when paper labels became common. Corkscrews,

which arrived along with bottle corks in the late seventeenth century (when they were described as 'steel Wormes') also formed part of the paraphernalia of serving wine.

Another important requirement was chilled glasses. A familiar contrivance was the scallop-rimmed monteith, in which several glasses could be cooled. A commentator in 1683 claimed that its name derived from 'a fantastical Scot called "Monsieur Monteigh" who at that time or a little before wore the bottoms of his cloake or coate so notched U U U U', a charming idea that has never been substantiated. Monteiths rapidly became common, and those of metal and with removable rims often doubled as punchbowls; silver examples were also used as race prizes. In France, an oval form of monteith, known as a *verrière*, was made in porcelain; and these became an essential component of the dessert service. From the mid-eighteenth century individual wine glass coolers, in which the bowl of the glass was upended in cold water, began to replace monteiths. One can be seen on the table in Alken's *The Toast* (see p.107). According to nineteenth-century household manuals, footmen were to place hock and champagne glasses in these coolers, and to put two wine glasses on the table before each diner.

It was considered impolite to drink without toasting (see pp.104–7). This could have disadvantages, as described by Prince Puckler-Muskau, who visited Britain in 1828: 'If the company is small, and a man has drunk to everybody but happens to wish for more wine, he must wait for dessert (after which he could drink freely), if he does not find himself in courage enough to brave customs.'

Opposite top: A 'jolly boat', a development of the bottle 'slider' for distributing wine round the table. More elaborate wheeled contraptions were also devised.

Opposite bottom: Glass is still preferred for serving wine, as silver both conceals its colour and imparts a taint.

Right: Bottle tickets, made in a variety of materials, identified the growing choice of drinks. Cider and 'small beer' often accompanied dinner.

Right: A monteith of 1709. Monteiths were being made in English creamware, possibly for export, as late as the 1790s.

'OF FISH, FOWL AND FRUIT ...'

The fashion for ceramics with naturalistic *trompe l'oeil* decoration intended to tease the eye can be traced back at least as far as the sixteenth century, when, working for a market that delighted in mannerist artifice, the French potter Bernard Palissy and his followers made dishes with decoration cast from real reptiles and fish. Similar pieces were also created by goldsmiths, but the potter had the distinct advantage of being able to use glaze pigments to render the natural colours of the flesh and scales moulded into his wares.

Naturalistically modelled and painted ceramics enjoyed a great vogue again in the middle of the eighteenth century, when such forms and decoration were much favoured by rococo designers. The Meissen factory probably initiated the vogue for *trompe l'oeil* serving vessels formed as fruit or vegetables, and by 1747 it was manufacturing small tureens or 'compotiers' formed as artichokes. Vigorously modelled vegetable and zoomorphic tureens were made at the French

faience factories of Strasbourg (between 1748 and 1754) and Sceaux, and the idea was enthusiastically taken up at the Chelsea and Longton Hall porcelain factories during the 1750s. Such English porcelain examples may have prompted Staffordshire potters to make teawares moulded as cauliflowers and pineapples in the following decade.

Although formed as cabbages, fish, or other foodstuffs served during the savoury courses, the smaller Chelsea vessels of this type – like Meissen's artichokes – were intended for use in the dessert. We know this from Benjamin Franklin, who bought 'Melons and Leaves' of English porcelain to serve cream and fruit, and from contemporary sales catalogues. One lot in a Chelsea sale catalogue of 1755, for example, consisted of a 'compleat service for the desart'

comprising 'a large cabbage leaf and bason, two vine leav'd dishes and four small sunflower leaves' (which suggests that the taste for uniform design for ceramic services was not then universal). The vogue for naturalistically moulded dry sweetmeats and ices, pressed in carved wooden moulds and often formed as fish, fruit or vegetables, was then at its height, and Chelsea's naturalistically modelled wares would have sat well on the table alongside such confectioners' conceits.

The fashion for such *trompe l'oeil* wares has been revived several times since the mid-eighteenth century, notably in Italy and Portugal in the late eighteenth and mid-nineteenth centuries (in tin-glazed earthenware), and at Coalport and Staffordshire around 1830 (in porcelain). Reviving a theme first explored at Strasbourg and Sceaux, most of these later examples are formed as dishes naturalistically modelled and painted with nuts, fruit, or vegetables. Such witty and elegant productions were either set out during the dessert or were possibly virtuoso pieces intended solely for display.

AFTER
DINNER

TOASTS AND LOVING CUPS, 1640–1830

The custom of reinforcing a wish with an alcoholic drink, made yet more effective by sharing it with others, is probably as old as the invention of alcohol itself. Certainly, when the Normans invaded England in 1066 they found the Danish-speaking community still using the old Norse toast 'ves heill' ('be of good health'), a custom so deep-rooted that eventually, evolving into 'Wassail', it became firmly attached to festivities on the Old Christmas Eve or Twelfth Night. In 1494 the Household Ordinances of Edward IV described how the chapel choir sang 'Wassell!' after ceremonial cups of spiced wine were presented to the King and Queen to close the festivities. By the early seventeenth century wassailing had moved from court to the street and to public houses, where it was noted later by Samuel Pepys. It also survived in remote country areas where the ancient annual custom was reinvented as an indispensable part of modern Christmas.

The wassail bowl itself, essentially intended for communal drinking, is related to the medieval wooden mazer. From the early seventeenth century elaborate cups were being made by skilled turners from rare hardwoods such as lignum vitae, with special compartments in the lid for exotic spices. The much cheaper slipware versions made in Staffordshire and the West Country after about 1680 reflect the drink's widening social position. In Wales the last dated bowl, with its domed lid and traditional 18 handles for passing the huge pot around, was made in 1892.

Spiced warm ale with roasted apples – 'lamb's wool' – bobbing on the surface formed the basic ingredients of a drink intended to dispel the penetrating coldness of December. But there were alternative hot alcoholic drinks that could be consumed throughout the winter. A dictionary of household vessels compiled between 1663 and 1682 includes 'possett pott or wassell cup or a sallibube, having two handles, with a pipe on the side', a description that matches the 'spowte pott' recorded as early as 1590.

Whilst syllabub was a cold dessert, made frothy with milk 'under the cow', posset could be both food and drink and was served hot. A thin posset was merely hot sweet spiced ale or cider curdled with milk, but the addition of 15 eggs to 3 pints (1.7 litres) of this hot liquor produced something akin to a warm alcoholic crème caramel, a sack posset, to be spooned and the dregs sucked through the spout. As a winter

The *Humpen* was a voluminous cylindrical glass popular for communal beer drinking in Central Europe and Germany.

drink, and sometimes served as a restorative for late-night revellers, posset survived until the end of the eighteenth century.

In country areas, and guilds and clubs – and independently of the annual wassail – the custom of passing round large multi-handled cups survived almost until the discovery of germs might have rendered it socially unacceptable. At Wrotham in Kent three-handled slipware 'tygs' were made from the 1620s, and Staffordshire potters produced much grander slip-trailed versions from later in the century until early in the eighteenth. The final development may be seen in the austere salt-glazed stoneware loving cups made in Nottingham and Derbyshire between 1700 and 1871, most of which are inscribed for presentation or specifically as wedding presents.

Feasting in the late medieval period involved much ceremony, symbolism and protocol, an integral part of which was the status conferred on the host by the grandness of his silver-gilt goblet. In Germany, such goblets were sometimes fancifully modelled as animals or birds with detachable heads and were used as 'welcome cups' offered to honoured-guests. A traveller in 1607 noted that these were also displayed, like 'treasures of the church'. The many surviving elegant tall covered glass goblets engraved at Nuremberg in the late seventeenth and eighteenth centuries demonstrate a continuing tradition of ceremonial toasting in high social circles. At a less affluent but more egalitarian level, ceremonial banquets held by tradesmen's guilds involved the use of elaborately decorated communal glass vessels – notably the giant *Humpen* which effectively proclaimed their function with brightly enamelled scenes of craft activities or the guild's armorial bearings.

The Restoration of Charles II in 1660 brought with it an upsurge in English living standards and the adoption of new continental customs. Chinese porcelain and Venetian glass was widely available, as were wines from all parts of Europe. During the eighteenth century dinner was taken early, often followed by drinking to excess, with the proposal of toasts used as an excuse. In 1716 the Bishop of Cork and Rosse condemned toasting as a 'great Evil'. In fact, toasts were not always enjoyable. On the one hand, a banquet attended by the Prince of Wales in about 1800 involved a party of Grenadiers firing volleys after each toast, and the calling of 23 'bumpers', during which 20 men consumed 63 bottles of

Set for wassail (spiced ale): the large bowl held ale and the smaller one the spices. Up-ended cups went over the vertical knobs.

The 'tyg' was an English form of shared drinking cup with multiple handles for passing it round.

TOASTS AND LOVING CUPS, 1640–1830

A Meissen punchbowl painted
with a punch-drinking scene
copied from William Hogarth's
*A Midnight Modern
Conversation.*

wine. On the other, a Frenchman dining in London in 1815 recounted suffering five solid hours of eating, after which the tablecloth was removed, the wine circulated, and the ladies retired to their tea and liqueur cordials, leaving the men to consume port and madeira until the desultory conversation altogether ceased. The growing propriety of Britain's middle classes after the self-indulgent Regency period ensured that such drinking would increasingly be confined to field sports, racing, gaming and gentlemen's clubs.

Clubs indeed provided the excuse for serious drinking among men of independent means. The various Jacobite clubs supporting the return of the Stuart dynasty are well known. Unsurprisingly, they seemed to flourish after 1746, when it became both safer to declare one's affiliation and also a completely lost cause. Similarly, the Freemasons had ceremonial utensils, including engraved 'firing glasses' for banging the table during toasts. Although eighteenth-century paintings of gentlemen drinking together often show orderly drinking with decent glasses and bottles of wine, it was not wine but fortified punch that became the favoured universal basis for drinking parties.

Around the punch bowl, the calling of toasts or bumpers varied widely, becoming more absurd and daring as inhibitions were relaxed. Apart from loyal toasts (which nobody could refuse) it was customary to name an absent lady, while the ladies present named an absent gentleman, followed by 'sentiments', which one writer described as 'generally a fatuous moral reflection'. Although the behaviour

shown in William Hogarth's *A Midnight Modern Conversation* (see p.72) would surely have been considered extreme, the deceptive sickly drink must have been responsible for many unfortunate remarks and severe headaches.

Unlike the native wassail and posset, punch was a foreign import that derived from the Persian *panj* or the Hindu *panch* – a reference to the drink's *five* ingredients. As a by-product of the trade with China in the 1660s, it was based on Arrack – raw spirit from Goa or Batavia – flavoured with sugar, lemon, lime, nutmeg and other spices. It rose to popularity in the 1680s when the first silver and delftware punchbowls were made. Soon massive bowls of heat-resistant Chinese porcelain were being imported, silver ladles with horn handles devised, and new recipes invented. Punch could be hot or cold, weak or strong, but always sweet and easy to drink to excess; and as a means of reinforcing friendships, it provided communal drinking without the need for shared drinking vessels.

Although few punch bowls were made in Britain after the 1820s, in a period of prosperity and resumption of the French wine trade, the custom did continue in country and sporting circles. As late as the 1920s published recipes for bottled punch were uncompromisingly alcoholic: 5 gallons (23 litres) Strong Brandy, 3 gallons (14 litres) Plain Syrup, tincture of lemon and orange peels, tincture of allspice and cloves. It is arguable that the well-established taste for exotic mixed drinks may have added to the popularity of the very latest fashion: cocktails.

Above: Elections prompted displays of loyalty on English drinking vessels, whether for ale or wine. The small glass has a thick foot for 'heeltaps' or banging on the table during toasts.

Left: Servants carry trays of wine and glasses; there are individual wine glass coolers and decanters on the table and bottles of wine in a cooler.

Tea, Coffee and Chocolate

*There was also at this time a Turkish drink to be solde,
almost in every street, called coffee, and a nother kind of
drink called Tee, and also a drink called Chocolate, which
was a very hearty drink.*

THOMAS RUGG, 1659

From the mid-seventeenth century, the new hot drinks – tea,
coffee and chocolate – had a profound effect on social
behaviour, creating an alternative to post-dinner drinking.
Their consumption demanded elaborate rituals and new
vessels for preparing and serving. Early patterns of
consumption have remained broadly unchanged up to the
present day. Tea, for example, became a mainstay of existence
in Britain, much less so in France, and barely drunk at all in
Germany and Spain, where coffee was far more popular. In
1734, less than a century after its introduction as a curious
eastern drink, Twinings' were importing 13,114 lb (5,948 kg)
of tea into Britain, as opposed to 5,137 lb (2,330 kg) of coffee
and a mere 2,897 lb (1,314 kg) of chocolate. High taxes,
however, ensured that tea remained the preserve of the well
off until 1784, when (following a series of bad harvests that
pushed up the price of ale, the staple drink of the poor)
British import duties were abolished. This was the catalyst for
a massive increase in tea drinking at all social levels,

Above: Part of a tile panel from
a London coffee house
showing an early conical coffee
pot in use. Coffee houses
offered the pleasures of
tobacco, alcohol and the
London newspapers.

Left: The women of the house
prepare tea on a lobed tray
similar to this delftware one. A
black servant carries a kettle to
refresh the pot.

The mother instructs her daughter on how to take hot chocolate, while she drinks coffee. The service combines porcelain, silver and lacquer.

equivalent to a pound a year per head of population by the end of the century.

Tea was introduced from China – first to Portugal in the sixteenth century and then to the Netherlands, from whence it was shipped to Britain during the mid-seventeenth century. Samuel Pepys had his first 'Cupp of Tee, a China drink', in 1660. Catherine of Braganza, Charles II's queen, confirmed it as a fashionable drink. Hailed as a panacea for all manner of ills, tea became a victim of its own popularity, with many commentators believing that its use would spread moral and physical decay. Even the *Gentleman's Magazine* warned 'against drinking tea too hot … which would thicken the blood' in 1750.

Elegance of presentation was essential, as the fashion for the new hot drinks went hand in hand with an increased emphasis on manners, conversation, etiquette and refined behaviour, and their popularity therefore inaugurated new social ceremonies, particularly for women. Tea was initially served after dinner – late afternoon in eighteenth-century

Britain – when it would be prepared in the drawing room by women; the men, meanwhile, would continue to enjoy their wine in the dining room until the company reunited for music, cards and conversation. This could last some time, and it thus became a focus for informal chat and the continuation of dinner table gossip. As Jane Austen reveals in *Pride and Prejudice* (1813), tea was also a prelude to other entertainment: 'When the gentlemen had joined them, and tea was over, the card tables were placed'. As dinner moved later in the day, tea began to be served beforehand, accompanied by bread or cake, becoming the forerunner of the mid-nineteenth-century 'afternoon tea' (which was served with the full panoply of sandwiches, cake and biscuits). Tea was also taken at assemblies, usually in a separate room, and it became popular at breakfast, as did coffee and chocolate. Indeed, chocolate could be taken almost anywhere, including, according to a French eighteenth-century engraving, in the bath. As many conversation pieces, portraits and literary accounts from the eighteenth and nineteenth centuries show, all three drinks were taken in bedrooms, boudoirs, salons and gardens – indeed wherever there was a social gathering, large or small – and increasingly at any time of day.

TEA, COFFEE AND CHOCOLATE

Part of a Niderviller cabaret set: matching *'déjeuners,'* or cabaret sets for up to four people, were popular for small parties.

Below: Tea and coffee pots have been made in novel or comical shapes since at least the 1740s. This porcelain coffee pot dates from 1862.

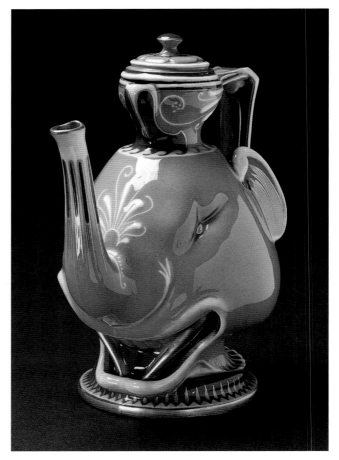

Coffee, widely drunk throughout the Middle East, was introduced to Europe by Turkish traders in the early seventeenth century. Although soon enjoyed as a domestic drink, it was initially popularized through coffee houses: Britain's first opened in Oxford in 1650 and London soon followed. These swiftly became places to gather, meet friends, do business, exchange news and read newspapers; and tea, sherbet, chocolate and mineral waters were also offered. Inevitably, they were seen as either pernicious, morally decadent places, or as essential for the continuance of the nation's social, economic and political life. In France, pedlars dressed as Turks sold coffee on the streets from trays equipped with coffee pot, cups and a stove; and the first coffee stall, set up in 1672, was the forerunner of French café society, also adopted in Germany, Italy and Portugal. Coffee became as ubiquitous in French society as tea in Britain. In 1782 the commentator Le Grand d'Aussy stated that there was 'no shopkeeper, no cook, no chambermaid who does not breakfast on coffee with milk … Women have set themselves up selling what they call *café au lait* to the populace, that is to say poor milk coloured with coffee grounds which they buy from the kitchens of big houses or café proprietors'.

Chocolate was a more costly drink and required greater preparation. Selling at first at 10 to 15 shillings per pound in England, it was perceived as a luxury and a food. Introduced from Mexico to Spain, it arrived in England in the 1650s. Chocolate 'cakes' were grated and sometimes boiled with claret, but were generally combined with eggs, milk, sugar, vanilla and spices, creating a mixture that requiring vigorous

Tea and coffee cups were usually pottery or porcelain (which did not get uncomfortably hot), even when the rest of the service was of silver.

whisking with a stirring rod, or 'molinet'. Medicinal properties were ascribed to the resultant brew, which was esteemed a 'great Cordial', one that 'restores lost strength [and] gives Appetite, wonderfully clearing the Spirits'.

The arrival of these new drinks created opportunities for manufacturers and importers of tablewares and ushered in new social rituals. All three could be drunk with milk, although the first tea to be introduced was green, or unfermented, which was generally taken without. Black, fermented tea was soon equally popular and later became even more so. Tea canisters were thus often supplied in pairs with the initials G and B (for Bohea, the most common black tea). The French, as described in an encyclopaedia of 1765, followed the Chinese method and diluted a strong brew with water after pouring. Small teapots could therefore be supplied with as many as 20 cups and saucers. Tea infused with lemon slices was also recommended, a method preferred to this day in France. Chocolate pots were

frequently distinguished by a handle set at 90 degrees to the spout, and those in silver often had a hinged knop to allow the insertion of a molinet. Cups and saucers were usually of pottery or porcelain, which were easier to handle than metal, as they did not get unpleasantly hot. There was a fashion for elegant lidded chocolate cups with two handles, which were often supplied in pairs as part of a fashionable toilet set. The tea equipage became more complex, including milk jug, sugar basin, slop bowl and, particularly from the 1760s, the hot water urn, as well as the tea tray and table. By the mid-eighteenth century manufacturers were supplying services combining tea and coffee equipment, and by the 1850s catalogues were offering a bewildering range of patterns, indicating how much the market had expanded. In Russia, tea had rapidly become a staple during the eighteenth century, and the invention of the samovar, a relation of the European hot water urn, ensured a constant supply of hot water as well as a warm place to set the pot to steep.

After-dinner Games and Pastimes

Left: The original Tom and Jerry, a rich man-about-town and his friend the country sportsman, being entertained by 'swell broad coves', from Pierce Egan's *Life in London* (1821).

Below: A fashionable crowd playing cards and Pope Joan at a party in 1796.

What does one do after dinner? Need one do anything, if it has been a good dinner? Byron recalled dining out 'with a large-ish party … of note and notoriety' in 1815. 'Like other parties of the kind, it was first silent, then talky, then argumentative, then disputatious, then unintelligible, then altogethery, then inarticulate, and then drunk. When we had reached the last step of this glorious ladder, it was difficult to get down again without stumbling.' Such Regency abandon was toned down in Victoria's reign, but, even then, enhanced socialization could be all that was required of a dinner party. A charming 'before and after' caricature of 1842 by George Cruikshank shows downcast guests waiting for dinner and the same group beaming and gesturing, 'whereby it seemeth clear / That people grow most cordial after dinner'.

Words were the prime entertainment at a dinner party, and after it. Wit and persiflage are best when spontaneous, but become constrained by etiquette, as in the late Victorian period: 'Too many anecdotes or too many jokes should be avoided,' ordered one manual; 'the propounder of conundrums should be removed by the police'. Literature could help if guests were short of ideas. Henry James told a correspondent in 1869 about visiting William Morris: 'After dinner … Morris read us one of his unpublished poems … and his wife, having a bad toothache, lay on the sofa, with her handkerchief to her face'. A more homely expedient is described in the diary of a country parson, Benjamin Robert Armstrong, in 1870: 'Conversation after dinner consisted of wonderful ghost stories'.

Music and dancing were traditional after-dinner amusements. While the rich had ballrooms, the not-so-rich had to extemporize. In 1870, Francis Kilvert, another country parson, recorded: 'After dinner the carpet was taken up in the drawing-room and there was a dance on the slippery dark oak floor'. Music could be provided by amateurs around the piano, or by hired professionals, or indeed as part of the table-service. After dining at Holland House in 1819, Tom Moore heard 'a very good male voice singing to the guitar' and found that 'it was the *butler* who was accompanying himself in an Italian air'.

Among those who could not sing or talk, card-playing became the conventional after-dinner entertainment, bridge and whist being most favoured. The illustration (above)

Above: 'The Passenger to Boulogne', an 'after-dinner entertainment' devised by Professor Hoffmann requiring only an orange, penknife, napkin and wine glass.

Below: 'The Rake at the Gaming Tables', from Rebecca West's *The Modern Rake's Progress* of 1934.

scores of other card games, from the old, like Pope Joan, which used a bank of counters on a board as well as cards, to the new, like poker, which reached England from the USA in the late nineteenth century. The first Director of the South Kensington Museum, Henry Cole, was an inveterate player of bezique.

In defiance of etiquette, the versatile guest might wish to equip himself (as advised in 'Professor' Hoffmann's *Drawing-Room Amusements*, 1879), with a few 'after-dinner accomplishments and more or less eccentric forms of amusement, which, when conversation chances to flag over "the walnuts and the wine" … may be employed to advantage'. These might involve making a tortoise out of a raisin or a pig out of a lemon, or placing an orange (carved with a miserable face) on a handkerchief over a wine glass. The handkerchief 'is then moved gently backwards and forwards over the top of the glass, imparting to the orange a rolling motion, and affording a laughable but striking caricature of the agonies of a sea-sick passenger.' The performance can be 'terminated by draping the pocket-handkerchief hood-fashion over the supposed head, and squeezing the orange into the glass', but Prof. Hoffmann deprecates this as 'disagreeably realistic'.

shows the original Tom and Jerry being entertained to dinner and whist by some 'swell broad coves' who are intent on winning their money by gambling. 'Inviting a man to a *swell* dinner, and making him pay *five guineas* a mouthful for it afterwards, is no new feature in *Life in London*.' There were

CELEBRATIONS
AND
CEREMONIES

❖

THE ROYAL TABLE IN ENGLAND

Left: The choreography of a court dinner was governed by strict rules: the dishes were brought in a procession under the direction of a major-domo and sometimes heralded by a trumpet blast.

Opposite above: The lack of privacy that characterized the royal requirement to dine surrounded by courtiers explains Charles II's preference for intimate suppers with his mistresses.

Opposite below: This bird's eye view of the King's table was published with a key to the list of dishes to celebrate the talents of the master cook and his team.

No person … shall presume to stand under Our Clothe of State … or lean upon the table after the salt is upon the table … Persons of good qualitie shall be suffered to remain in the chamber: & those shall stay towards the lower end of the chamber.

ORDINANCES FOR CHARLES I'S HOUSEHOLD, C.1631

Hospitality has always been one of the chief obligations of a monarch: from the earliest times, lavish and large-scale dinners enhanced his status and spread goodwill amongst his guests and subjects. The Stuarts retained the medieval ceremonial service by cup-bearers, carvers and sewers for their public dinners. They also retained such exclusive royal symbols as the king's salt, a casket shaped like a ship, supplemented by the caddinet for his cutlery, introduced by the Valois kings of France. The vital element was splendour – splendour in the form of the enormous variety of dishes served and the amount of gold or at least gilded plate displayed on the sideboards. However, as more royal dinners were eaten in private, much of the ritual and display disappeared. Mary Berry referred to the 'German homeliness' of the courts of the first two Georges, which altered little under George III. Their eldest son on becoming Prince Regent may have revived the earlier pomp, but his successors, William IV and Queen Victoria, preferred less ostentation.

King Charles I and Queen Henrietta Maria dined twice a week in the manner recorded by Gerrit Houckgeest in

Charles I Dining in Public. The table was still spread with a clutter of dishes brought in procession and uncovered as they were set down, in marked contrast to the table layouts of the Queen's brother, King Louis XIII of France: his table layers adopted elaborately symmetrical arrangements in the Italian manner. The King and Queen would have helped themselves to what was placed immediately in front of them, and sat alone, as Louis XIII did, attended by their highborn officers of state, serving in rota.

Following the Restoration of the Stuarts in 1660, both Charles II and his brother James II held public dinners after their coronations, which were described and illustrated by John Ogilby and Francis Sandford respectively. Both feasts were held in Westminster Hall; both sovereigns sat in isolation from their guests; and both underwent similar rituals, ranging from having their hands washed from a basin and ewer by the cup-bearer to witnessing the Champion riding in and throwing down the gauntlet to challenge opponents. However, unlike Ogilby, Sandford lists the dishes of the first course and shows how they were arranged on the tables. Prominent on the King's table were three pyramids, composed of lemons, bay leaves and sweetmeats, towering over 145 open dishes ranging from mangoes and Parmesan cheese to oyster pies and puffins. After a second course of 30 'hot meats', the King and Queen left. (Courses involved the clearing of one set of dishes from the table and replacing it with a second, usually a mixture of roasts, jellies and

The manner of Placeing the Meß on their Majesties Table (being 145 severall dishes The Figures directing to the Printed Catalog shewing what Meats were contained in each Dish

There were 30 dishes more served to their Majesties Table at the second Course.

sweetmeats.) Both sovereigns dined two or three times a week in public, but viewers were limited to 'Persons of Good Fashion and Good Appearance'. Samuel Pepys attended regularly, and on one occasion witnessed the King wiping pieces of bread on each dish and placing them in his cup-bearer's mouth, to test for poisoning. Like most European monarchs they looked to France and the court of Louis XIV for their model of regal splendour. At Versailles Louis regularly dined in public, but once he had finished and left, spectators were allowed to help themselves to what remained, something that seems not to have happened in England. Samuel Pepys was once invited to eat 'meat that came from [the King's] table' by the back stairs in Whitehall Palace.

Unlike his predecessors, William III had little taste for public dinners, and his sister-in-law, Queen Anne, was noted for her modest appetite. The Hanoverians had no tradition of public dining: George I spoke no English, and preferred to eat in private with his mistresses. However, his son the Prince and Princess of Wales ate publicly at St James's, where 'all sorts of people have free admission to see them, even the lowest sort'. Prince Frederick Louis ordered a number of silver services, the finest surviving piece being the Poseidon centrepiece by Paul Crespin (1741/2); George III, likewise, made major acquisitions of plate, notably a pair of French neoclassical tureens by Henri Auguste. However, George III preferred privacy and the company of his

THE ROYAL TABLE IN ENGLAND

Above: To promote the image of princely splendour, the set-up for a Carlton House dinner of 1811 was opened to thousands of visitors, just as Henry VIII had done in the 1520s.

Below: The theatricality and aggrandisement in Regency dining: as more guests attended, dining rooms became bigger and tables and sideboards groaned with plate.

consort, Queen Charlotte, and his table was described as 'neither sumptuous nor elegant'. By 1760, when he took the throne, both the king's salt and caddinet were obsolete, and stunning displays of silver and the silver-gilt plateaux with temples of gilt-wood or baked sugar would have to wait until his eldest son assumed the role of Prince Regent in 1811.

In this year the Prince Regent acquired Louis XVI's porcelain service, made for Versailles between 1783 and 1792. He also made unprecedented large purchases of silver from Rundell, Bridge & Rundell between 1812 and 1819, ranging from eight large ice pails modelled on the Warwick Vase, and a sideboard dish depicting the Feast of the Gods based on a design of Michelangelo, to a Gothic 'Black Prince Plateau'. Under the Prince Regent, French chefs such as Antonin Carême, and French dishes held sway over the royal kitchens. From 1812, menus included 'Quinels [Quenelles] of Fowl à la Richelieu', 'Mackrells aux fines herbes', 'Fillets of Soles en Papillote' and countless others (albeit with ever fewer Anglicisms) harking back to the olios, fricassees and

The Prince of Wales' dining room at Sandringham, *c*.1890. Note the simple folding of the napkins at a time when elaborate arrangements were fashionable.

ragouts of James II's celebrations. Royal receptions took on a new brilliance, and few could have been more spectacular than one of 1811, held in the Gothic Conservatory of Carlton House, in honour of the exiled King Louis XVIII of France. An engraving depicts, with satirical comments, the inventive table centrepiece in the form of a stream flowing with live silvered and gilded fish, and shows Yeomen of the Guard protecting a buffet displaying plate borrowed from the Tower.

The Prince Regent's greatest reception was the dinner in Westminster Hall after his coronation as King George IV in July 1821. Some 2,000 were invited and 3,903 dishes laid out. The sideboards either side of the throne were bedecked with seventeenth- and eighteenth-century gilded plate, and much of the ritual was borrowed from Charles II's and James II's coronation banquets, including the mounted Champion (although this time on a horse trained by Astley's Circus).

The King's table was decorated with gilt pasteboard temples, which were torn apart once the spectators were 'admitted to partake of such refreshments as remained on the tables' and ended up filching whatever souvenir they could.

George IV's niece, Queen Victoria, retained an unreserved enthusiasm for the porcelain of Herbert Minton throughout her life; and his younger brother, William IV, made a number of highly important orders, such as his Coronation Service by Flight, Barr and Barr of Worcester, and the Rockingham Service, designed by John Wagner Brameld, in celebration of Britain's naval prowess. When it came to dining, Victoria's menus were predominantly French, but her luncheons included at least one German dish, no doubt to cater for the Prince Consort. Her dinners were seldom, if ever, divided into the traditional first and second courses. Earlier in her reign the (by now) one course consisted of different soups, followed by fish, entrées, relevées (removes), roasts and entremets (a mixture of savouries and puddings) with other roasted meats on the side table. By the 1890s, there was considerably less variety: only four entremets and two of *entrées*, removes and roasts would have been the norm.

THE VICTORIAN CHRISTMAS DINNER

The first Christmas card, 1843: this scene of Victorian Christmas cheer was frowned upon by contemporary temperance societies.

Below: A Victorian Christmas pudding plate bordered with dancing bottles and barrels; the donkey is a curious choice as it is normally associated with Easter.

In 1843 three essential elements were added to the magic of Christmas: the creation of the first Christmas card, the introduction of what Charles Dickens described as that 'pretty German toy, a Christmas Tree', and the publication of *A Christmas Carol*, Dickens's Christmas story.

The idea for the first Christmas card came to a dynamic young man at the Patent Office, the future Sir Henry Cole, one of the great innovators of his time, who is remembered today for creating the Great Exhibition, the Crystal Palace, and the precursors of the Victoria and Albert Museum and Science Museum. For such a man 'networking' was vital, and when he tired of the task of writing Christmas letters, Cole commissioned a pictorial greeting card from an artist friend John Calcott Horsely, both for personal use and general sale.

The main panel of the card shows a Victorian family lunch party. The gathering is toasting the health of absent friends, such as the recipient of the card. All drink red wine, with the exception of the three smallest children, who taste the plum pudding. The side panels reflect the spirit of Christmas charity, showing the poor being fed and given warm clothing. The conviviality of the central group was however frowned upon by advocates of abstinence from alcohol, the temperance societies, who criticized the card for 'encouraging drunkenness'. In 1845 perhaps to appease such speculations Cole won a prize offered by the Society for Arts for the design of a tea-service, thus promoting a non-alcoholic beverage. But alcohol was an essential ingredient in that key element of the Christmas dinner – the Pudding, amusingly described in Dickens's *A Christmas Carol*:

Hallo! A great deal of steam! The pudding was out of the copper. A smell like a washing day! … the pudding, like a speckled cannon ball, so hard and firm, blazing in half of half-a-quartern of ignited brandy, and bedight with Christmas holly stuck into the top. 'There never was such a pudding!' said Tiny Tim.

Turkey had been recommended for Christmas festivities by Thomas Tusser as early as 1573, and Jane Austen mentions eating it at Christmas in 1812, when many still preferred the more traditional roast beef; but by Dickens' time turkey was the clear favourite. Although he loved the profusion of Christmas, Dickens disliked vulgar *nouveau riche* ostentation, a prominent theme in *Our Mutual Friend* (1865), which includes this vivid description of Victorian plate of the type that would have been used at many Victorian Christmas dinners:

Hideous solidity was the characteristic of the Podsnap plate. Everything was made to look as heavy as it could, and to take up as much room as possible. Everything said boastfully 'here you have as much of me in my ugliness as if I were only

A colonial Christmas meal of steaming plum pudding and fruit enjoyed *al fresco*.

MAY CHRISTMAS BE THY HARBINGER OF JOY!

Prospects of a Good Time: a table set with jellies and plum pudding, from the sketchbook of amateur artist Charlie Hammond.

lead; but I am so many ounces of precious metal worth so much an ounce; – wouldn't you like to melt me down?' All the big silver spoons and forks widened the mouths of the company expressly for the purpose of thrusting the sentiment down their throats with every morsel they ate.

Although far more humble, a much more enjoyable impression of the wonder of the tree, the pudding and the table, can be seen in Charlie Hammond's *Prospects of a Good Time*, shown here. As a youth Hammond emigrated to Australia, but looked back in such drawings at happy childhood memories. Like Marcel Proust's *madeleine*, the Christmas pudding could also act as a stimulant 'for memories of times past', as it does in a Christmas card of about 1860 showing a pig-tailed servant holding a blazing pudding aloft at an expatriate Christmas picnic – somewhere 'East of Suez'.

DINING AWAY FROM HOME

The picnic basket of today – lovingly compacted to carry both delicious food and the napkins, glasses (not plastic), plates and cutlery to consume it – captures the values associated with formal dining. Refinement, elegance and luxury are still recognizable, just as they were in the lavish rock crystal and gold banqueting service that Henry VIII carried on his journeys to Calais, or the travelling sets of eighteenth-century aristocrats. A handsome wooden chest, intended for a duchess of Bedford in 1786 and preserved at Woburn, includes porcelain cups and saucers and a silver tea equipage with a kettle on a stand complete with a windshield. A set in a travelling box, supplied by Charles Asprey of Bond Street for a Portuguese princess in the 1860s, contains flatware slotted onto baize-lined pullout trays, silver food boxes, crystal glass decanters and impedimenta for tea and coffee. This travelled in the royal *charàbanc* between Lisbon and the summer palaces.

Prince Potemkin, a Russian grandee of great wealth who travelled incessantly, 'did not stint himself on food during his travels and consumed with great appetite both the most expensive viands such as fish soup at 1300 roubles from a silver bath … as well as the most simple cakes and biscuits.' The 'bath' is in fact a superb English silver wine cooler of 1699 weighing 112 kg – a curiously ostentatious choice of vessel for soup, and one that he set out, again full of fish soup, at his great victory party for 150 guests in 1791.

European princes habitually travelled with bottles of wine in silver *caves*, devised to ensure the safety of the bottles, and a suitably noble container for service on the road. These objects are rare, although one from the early eighteenth century can be seen in the Residenz, Munich, and a similar piece is depicted in the border of the Marlborough tapestries. These borders show all the travelling equipment essential for a royal general and are a reminder that the niceties of aristocratic eating were seen as a necessity even on the battlefield. James II had a 700-oz silver vessel made 'to carry His Majesty's Meat in the Field' during manoeuvres in 1688; and even in the darkest years of the First World War, the Emperor of Austria's dining car travelled with its full complement of porcelain and silver.

Where could people eat away from home? If travelling without a large entourage, private rooms were available at

Left: The constraints of dining etiquette were relaxed out of doors. The linen recalls the sacramental origins of a shared meal in a licentious atmosphere.

Right: Toasting the Dauphin: loyal citizens at an improvised dinner break the 18th-century etiquette of decorum.

Right: Again, the tablecloth unites the company sprawled uncomfortably around a dry repast.

THE PICNIC, (EPPING FOREST.)

inns, where a meal could be commanded. The easy choice offered in restaurants today and the diversity of ready food available in every high street is a recent phenomenon. Until the mid-eighteenth century, and the emergence of the restaurant with a changing menu, people had essentially three choices: to go to an 'ordinary' where a dish of the day, bread and a drink were provided for a set price; to buy ready-prepared food from a cook shop or traiteur; or to seek an invitation from an acquaintance. However, the several new urban 'pleasure gardens', such as Vauxhall or Ranelagh, offered specific menus, which were in themselves novel; here women of refinement could be entertained without losing their reputations.

Generally, four spits, one over another, carry round each five or six Pieces of Butchers Meat … you have what quantity

DINING AWAY FROM HOME

The restaurant, offering delicious choice of food and drink with no trouble except the bill, was invented in Paris in the 1750s.

you please cut off, fat, lean, much or little done. With this, a little Salt and Mustard upon the side of a Plate, a Bottle of Beer and a Roll; and there is your whole Feast.

This concept of the London 'ordinary', described so vividly by the French traveller M. Misson in the 1690s and revived by Sibyl Colefax at the Dorchester in the 1940s, was an alternative to the hospitality still offered in the early eighteenth century by the Board of Green Cloth at St James's Palace, and the Archbishop of Canterbury at Lambeth Palace, and enjoyed by Conrad von Uffenbach in 1710. Otherwise the ancient idea of English country hospitality, 'keeping open house' with simple food and drink offered to any respectable traveller, gradually died during the seventeenth century. It was killed partly by its cost and the economic pressures on the rural gentry during and after the Civil War, but also because of the appeal of a simpler life in London and of a retreat into privacy and gentility. However,

when Georgian aristocrats such as Sir Robert Walpole at Houghton returned for the autumn season to their country estates, they held 'public days', which local gentry were encouraged to attend. The food offered was less than a dinner but more than bread and cheese, and the discharge of social obligations was mutually acknowledged. Traces remain today in country towns of the old social rhythms; a more elaborate menu, heavy with roast meat, is still offered on market days, even if the market itself has dwindled to a few stalls selling vegetables, cheap textiles and compact discs.

Hunting and shooting parties both demanded hearty food, and Edwardian photographs show lavish arrangements of damask-covered tables set up in the field and served with all the ceremonial appropriate to a dining room. A woodcut of Elizabeth I in the hunting field shows her seated at a tablecloth spread on the grass, alone as royal etiquette demanded, and enjoying a similar ritual presentation of her wine and food as when dining in public at Greenwich or Whitehall. The Danish court owns a set of eighteenth-century silver tureens, crowned with boars, hunting horns and stags, which were designed for forest lodge dinners.

Hungry people lacking a settled home life applied ingenuity to creating meals without a kitchen. In the 1730s John Rich, pantomime actor at Covent Garden, devised the Necromancer, a means to prepare 'Thin-beef Collups Stew'd' in wine in his private room at the theatre, without a fire. 'You may do this Dish between two pewter Dishes, hang them between two Chairs, take six sheets of White-Brown Paper, tare them into slips and burn them under the Dish one piece at a time'. After 15 minutes 'Your Stew will be enough, and full of Gravy', as Hannah Glasse explained.

In the summer syllabubs and sweetened creams, with fruit, were enjoyed in tavern gardens in the late seventeenth century. These popular refreshments, like the new beverages of tea, coffee and chocolate, exploited the increasing availability of refined sugar from the West Indies. In the 1660s, playing at dairymaids, Lady Castlemaine was walking with Charles II in St James's Park and called for a large porcelain basin with white wine and sugar. She milked a cow into the mixture and the delicious froth was then shared. Although sweetened de-fatted chocolate bars became a commercial product only in the mid-nineteenth century, Dutch 'tablets' or 'cakes' of chocolate were sold in London in the 1660s, and advertised as a source of nourishment for travellers. Prepared with sugar and spices, the 'cake' could be scraped into powder and made into a sweet rich drink with either wine or milk and water. Sugar in all its forms was an increasingly important part of the English national diet. In 1734 an economist calculated that the London 'middling sort' spent a seventh of their budget for food and drink on tea and sugar, supplemented by bread.

Pullman travellers enjoyed in miniature all the pleasures of formal dining, including fine linen, liveried waiters, table decorations and a Turkey carpet.

The shared tables of an inexpensive restaurant demonstrate the conviviality and lack of intimacy typical of eating out a century ago, just as today.

Dining with the Duke of Wellington

The Duke of Wellington's momentous victory at Waterloo in 1815 finally ended the threat posed by Napoleon across Europe, and Britain's allies showered the Duke with gifts in gratitude. Perhaps the most spectacular were the Meissen, Berlin, Vienna and Sèvres dinner services, which together comprise the most striking assemblage of early nineteenth-century continental porcelain in Britain. Along with three silver services presented to the Duke, these remain at Apsley House, his London residence, which was the setting for his most lavish entertaining – the annual banquets held to celebrate the anniversary of his greatest victory.

On campaign, Wellington described his dinners as 'no great things'. One, in September 1813, consisted of white soup and boiled fish; mutton and roast beef; 'made' dishes including a 'very good' one with rice and apples; a dessert of apples, stewed peaches and walnuts, all served on plate and a 'fashionably wide' table. His personal tastes were simple: he had wine, champagne and black tea shipped out from England; but, on his own, he might take dinner 'walking about munching' and survive during the day on a crust of bread and a boiled egg in his pocket. Cold meat was usually served, although a hot dinner was specially requested after Waterloo.

In England, the Duke often entertained at Stratfield Saye House, Hampshire. When Queen Victoria stayed in 1845, the Duke piled her plate high with pudding and tarts all mixed

Right: View of the Waterloo banquet of 1836 showing the Portuguese plateau, but without its candelabra, which would have hidden some of the sitters.

Below: The Waterloo Gallery with the dining table (seating 85) and side-tables set out with cutlery and plates for the Duke's last banquet in 1852.

together – much to her amusement. In London the Duke built a new dining room and, downstairs, displayed his plate and porcelain in glass-fronted mahogany cases, a visual feast for his guests that he may have copied from the Prince Regent.

The Duke travelled widely, knew Paris well, and associated closely with royalty. The Prince Regent set the fashion for the most ostentatious and lavish entertaining. Foreigners were struck by the 'profusion of solid and sumptuous plate upon the tables'. Visual spectacle was all-important and was a major feature of the Waterloo banquets. Newspapers were effusive; in 1838 the *Morning Post* reported: 'On entering the picture gallery the effect is extraordinary … literally one blaze of gilding … At each end … are sideboards, where a quantity of gold and silver plate is arranged in dazzling profusion'.

The Waterloo banquets were held at Apsley House every year (though at Downing Street in 1829) until the Duke's death in 1852. As only 36 diners could be accommodated in the Dining Room, the Duke decided in 1828 to add on the spectacular Waterloo Gallery, which seated 85.

The Duke made full use of the sumptuous services presented to him: Berlin porcelain from Frederick William III of Prussia; Meissen from Frederick Augustus I of Saxony; Vienna from Francis I of Austria; and Sèvres from Louis XVIII of France (see also pp.88, 95), as well as the silver service of over 1,000 pieces, with its outstanding 7.92-m (26-ft) long centrepiece, given by the Portuguese government (see pp.114–15). The public was admitted with passes to see the Waterloo banquets set up and spectators thronged the streets to witness guests arriving.

The several services were laid out together and adapted by the Duke. Silver salts from the Deccan Service and waiters on wheels from the Ambassador Service were used alongside porcelain. The Duke commissioned salt cellars, sauce tureens and fish-servers from Garrard and Storr to supplement the Portuguese Service, as well as hot plates and stands to keep the food warm. Ever practical, he had the centrepiece adapted so that fewer sections could be used.

The Prussian Service was the only porcelain service to include a complete set of serving dishes and matching dinner

DINING WITH THE DUKE OF WELLINGTON

plates, of which there were originally 100. The centrepiece comprises several of the largest pieces, its highlight being a huge obelisk surrounded by biscuit (unglazed) figures of gods of rivers connected to the Duke. The dessert plates have exquisitely painted scenes reflecting the Duke's life.

For the Waterloo banquets, guests arrived 6.30–7.30 p.m. King William IV was guest of honour in 1836. In later years the Prince Consort often attended, being greeted by the Duke under the portico. The band of the Grenadier Guards played music as guests entered, just before and during dinner and in between the numerous toasts – often nearing a dozen. In 1843 the music included Rossini, a grand march, a waltz and a quadrille. (For other dinners at Apsley House the Duke hired a piano and musicians. In 1831 Charles Greville remarked on 'Styrian Minstrels playing and

The obelisk from the Berlin Service, inscribed with Wellington's titles, surrounded by biscuit porcelain river gods.

singing all dinnertime, a thing I never saw before'. The banquets ended at about 10.30 p.m. and guests had departed by 11.00 p.m.

Flowers and plants were displayed in abundance, including, in 1849, 'two luxuriant dwarf vines, bearing a superfluity of fruit of the most exuberant culture ... and some enormous pines'. Garlands of silk flowers linked the hands of the dancing nymphs of the Portuguese centrepiece. Candlelight from the central chandelier and two magnificent Russian torchères, which the table fitted around, created a stunning effect with the mirrored walls and silver centrepiece.

As to food, a menu of 1839 written by a French chef, testifies just how lavish the dinners, when presented *à la française*, could be. Two different soups, one for each end of the table, were accompanied by four fish dishes and four savoury *relevées*, and then by 24 *entrées* (including 'made' dishes with pigeon, veal, duckling and lamb). Four roasts and two lots of four *relevées*, in due course replaced these, to be followed by 24 entremets (a real mixture of sweet and savoury including lobster salad, plovers' eggs, petits pois, artichokes, asparagus, pineapple ices and strawberry charlotte). Dishes on the side table included roast beef, saddle of mutton and venison for the first course and apple and gooseberry tarts for the second.

The Duke hired extra equipment for grander occasions. A bill of 1815 from the goldsmiths Garrards' includes 24 wine labels and 24 teaspoons, and one of 1844 lists 36 table-forks and tablespoons, 24 teaspoons and assorted candlesticks. Another bill for June 1838 – presumably for the Waterloo banquet – covered 'Taking up the carpets, removing all the Furniture in Gallery, laying down Damask Drugget, fitting up Dining tables, Side Tables, taking up Carpets, oil cloth, Druggets in Drawing Room and Passages, taking down Dining Tables and replacing the furniture &c &c £15.16.0 ... 36 Mahogany Dining Room chairs £3.12.0 ... 2 dozen Trussels 12s ... 150 feet of Caned Seats'.

Food bills mounted up. The Duchess managed the accounts, but the Duke sometimes took a surprisingly close interest. In 1820 he wrote a memorandum to his wife: 'Fishmongers is a most extravagant bill ... What is the meaning of 18 lemons costing 15 shillings one day and 12 lemons costing 9 shillings the next?' The Duchess eventually sacked their chef, James Thornton, for extravagance, after several instructive observations including: 'In every family ... made Dishes which are but little touched at one Dinner are served up again ... while but one day intervenes'.

The Waterloo banquets were almost on a par with entertaining at court. They represented the very grandest dining of the time, attracting wide interest. They were private, but also national, well-publicized celebrations.

A soup tureen from the Portuguese Service: the band of Minerva's shields refers to Perseus' release of Andromache, and by extension to Wellington's victories.

A *sucrier* from the Egyptian Service, surely one of the most flamboyant and elegant sugar bowls ever made.

Dessert plate from the Saxon Service painted with a view of Apsley House.

DINING AT THE RITZ

Left: The Ritz Restaurant in 1906, during its heyday before the First World War.

Below: Supper at the Ritz in 1925: the Ritz had cachet, reliability and a restaurant that combined grandeur with intimacy.

As soon as it opened in 1906, the Ritz Hotel in Piccadilly was adopted by high society. It constituted the apotheosis of the Swiss hotelier, César Ritz (1850–1918), who was enticed to London in 1889 as first manager of D'Oyly Carte's Savoy Hotel. Working with the chef Auguste Escoffier, after 10 years he had won the English over to the concept of eating in public restaurants, to late night and Sunday opening and, above all, to French *haute cuisine*. The hotel named after him aspired to even higher standards.

Built in Beaux-Arts style by the architectural partnership of Mewès and Davis, the Ritz had sumptuous Louis-Seize-revival interiors – supplied by Waring and Gillow – which flattered guests with a softer, more feminine ambiance. The restaurant was lined with pastoral murals and polychrome marble panels; pink clouds drifted across the blue sky of the *trompe l'oeil* ceiling. The bronze chandeliers were linked by bronze flower garlands, so the room appeared to be permanently *en fête*. At one end a marble buffet supported large gilded lead figures representing Neptune and a sea nymph. The silver came principally from Christofle of Paris, the plate from Elkington and the china from Royal Doulton. Glowing with electric candelabra at night or bathed in daylight from the French windows overlooking Green Park, it was – and still may be – the most beautiful dining room in London.

The food lived up to the promise of the setting. Escoffier was consulted but the chef principally responsible was M. Malley, assisted by a specialist in Russian soups and a Viennese pastry cook. He invented new dishes, such as *Saumon Marquise de Sévigné* (salmon with crayfish mousse) and *Filet de Sole Romanoff* (sole with mussels, apples and artichokes), far removed from heavy, masculine, English fare. Significantly, according to Lady Diana Cooper it was the first hotel where young unmarried women could be seen unchaperoned.

The heyday of the Ritz was before the First World War. King Edward VII would dine with his last mistress, Mrs Keppel, in the private Marie Antoinette Suite. The German and Austrian embassies retained a table for all meals. But with the loss of this regular clientele, not to mention key staff suddenly deemed enemy aliens, the hotel's fortunes

Left: The Ritz Restaurant still evokes the richness and delicacy associated with 18th-century French interiors.

Below: A menu of the year 2000 offering medallions of lamb, roast squab pigeon, seared sea bass, chilled sole Duglère, or risotto of roast tomatoes for lunch.

The Ritz Restaurant

foundered and it was even fined for breaking Food Control Orders. Nevertheless, it was able to celebrate the Armistice in 1918 with a Victory Dinner, featuring such specialities as *Filets de Sole Maréchal Haig*.

To the Bright Young People of the 1920s, the Ritz stood for rather stuffy standards, as illustrated by a passage from Evelyn Waugh's *Vile Bodies* (1930): '"Of course there's always the Ritz," said Archie. "I believe the night porter can usually get one a drink." But he said it in the sort of voice that made all the others say, no, the Ritz was too, too boring at that time of night.'

However, it had some advantages over noisy clubs such as the Embassy: cachet, reliability and a restaurant that combined grandeur with intimacy. Waugh himself used the Ritz all his life, to impress others – here he proposed to his

first wife over dinner – and for his own pleasure, dubbing the hotel 'marble halls' in his letters. It was also the smart place for ladies to lunch; the set price was 8s 6d compared with 17s 6d for a five-course dinner. In 1934 Lady Furness took Mrs Ernest Simpson to luncheon at the Ritz, asking her to look after Edward, Prince of Wales, while she was away abroad. The rest is Abdication history.

During the Second World War, the Ritz managed to stay open, its steel frame thought to provide safe shelter. A snack bar was installed next to the basement Grill Room. Having fled from Italy, Mrs Keppel returned to the Ritz in 1940 and stayed until she died in 1947. Her great grand-daughter, Camilla Parker Bowles, was seen for the first time in public with the present Prince of Wales, leaving a party at the Ritz in 1999.

DRESSING THE CORPORATE TABLE

The dining table has always been an arena for the display and exercise of power, wealth, confidence and taste being expressed through the scale, design and diversity of silver. However, institutions achieve splendid effects differently from private individuals.

In Max Beerbohm's fictional account of an Oxford college dinner the dessert is served in hall, after the removal of the tablecloth, revealing 'a clear dark lake … to reflect in its still and ruddy depths the candelabra and the fruit-cradles, the slender glasses and the stout old decanters, the forfeit box and the snuff-box, and other paraphernalia of the dignity of dessert'. The photograph here shows an alternative college custom, retiring to a separate room for dessert for more informal talk. This setting at New College Oxford reveals how seventeenth- to twentieth-century dining wares are combined to create an overall effect of plenty, linking the past to the present. On the central table sits a nineteenth-

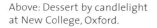

Above: Dessert by candlelight at New College, Oxford.

Right: The traditional panelled setting of the Luncheon Room at Goldsmiths' Hall contrasts with the contemporary flatware and recent commissions displayed on the table.

Kevin Coates' St George and the Dragon Centrepiece combines vibrant colours with traditional heraldic ornament crowned by England's patron saint.

century epergne loaded with grapes, flanked by a pair of Victorian gilt *tazze* in Renaissance style, and one of the silver cake baskets filled with fruit is eighteenth-century. On each of the six circular side tables stands an eighteenth-century candlestick. The table at the back bears nineteenth-century decanters, eighteenth-century coasters, a bottle opener from the Jensen workshop and a snuffer by the Oxford silversmith Stella Campion.

What unites these disparate objects is the fact that they each bear an inscription in memory of the donor, with his name, and often armorials, and the date of the gift. Through the tableware donors have a lasting presence within the college. The taking of dessert is governed by ritual, the Sub-Warden, or most senior college member present, sits at the left-hand table, circulating bottles and decanters, while the most junior serve the fruits, nuts and chocolates. Snuff is then offered, and coffee served in the adjoining Smoking Room. As one Fellow remarked, the smooth running of the

procedure depends on the experience of those attending, and at one notable event the new Sub-Warden kept the bottles circulating so liberally that all guests failed to make it to coffee.

The eclectic mix familiar to a college or livery company finds fresh expression in today's emphasis on creative diversity in design. Although the early twentieth century saw a decline in the commissioning of new plate, in favour of purchasing antique, the last 50 years have seen a resurgence in the crafts, the 1990s witnessing a positive renaissance in silver tableware in Britain. This has been largely driven by the Goldsmiths' Company, the Crafts Council and individual initiatives to promote the talents and abilities of today's makers through exhibitions and commissions.

One of the earliest, and most ambitious, commissioning campaigns of the last decade centred on the idea of creating a national collection of silver, made possible by a generous gift towards the end of 1990. Central to this was the

DRESSING THE CORPORATE TABLE

commission by the Silver Trust of a dinner service for diplomatic use, in order to encourage and publicise the work of contemporary British silversmiths. By early 1993 there was sufficient silver to present the collection to Downing Street for use by the Prime Minister. Today there are over 300 pieces in the collection, representing the work of 96 artists, designers and goldsmiths. The service, which tours frequently on exhibition, provides a snapshot of the astonishing range of skills and approaches to design of modern British silversmiths: from the highly modelled and jewel-like work of Kevin Coates, demonstrated in his St George Centrepiece shown here, to the simple sculptural elegance of Keith Redfern's highly polished jugs. The dinner service remains in regular use for government and state occasions.

The commissioning of these one-off pieces was accompanied by a competition offering artists, designers, and members of the public the opportunity to design a pattern for a 20-oz spun silver under-plate. Although no firm guidelines were given, it was suggested that the designs might include the heraldic emblems of the United Kingdom or relevant national themes. The 72 winning designers, many of them amateurs, were chosen by a panel of judges from over 500 applicants. Each plate was individually sponsored by private and corporate donation.

London has not been alone in rejuvenating the dinner service as a potent symbol of faith in the future. As Scotland entered a new era, with the nation's Parliament sitting for the first time in 300 years, the Scottish Goldsmiths' Trust began commissioning one of the largest collections of modern silver, intended for the First Minister of Scotland's entertainments at ute House. By April 2001 all 15 silversmiths had completed r pieces: Malcolm Appleby has devised and created a centre drawing on Scottish heraldry, Michael Lloyd buted a pair of water jugs, and the er Maureen Edgar made a condiment g the work of these well-known younger smiths, such as Grant o graduated in 1998. In addition ff pieces is a limited edition of s and accompanying first set will remain at Bute being sold for the aft. Designed and made Hamilton and Inches of ent the skills and trade, and

al

incorporate a lion rampant, the traditional Scottish heraldic beast and the symbol for sterling silver in Scotland. The collection projects an image of confidence, innovation, design skills and dexterity.

Similar ambitions led to the creation of the Sheffield Millennium Canteen, which was commissioned by Sheffield City Council in 1991 to celebrate 600 years of cutlery manufacture in the city. All 37 contributors are members of the Association of British Designer Silversmiths, who seek to stimulate commissions for contemporary work. Made as an exhibition piece, rather than for the dinner table, the 74-piece canteen is a vehicle for radical design solutions and superlative craftsmanship, which triumph here over the practical requirements of use.

Concentrating on these recent large-scale corporate commissions misrepresents the more gradual adoption of new designs within older institutions. City livery companies, like older university colleges, retain long traditions of ceremony and ritual, expressed in their tableware and the customs for which they are used. At the Goldsmiths' Hall the Court dines in splendour surrounded by the Company silver, representing the work of its freemen from the sixteenth to the present century. Since 1957 the Company has given each newly elected member of its Court of Assistants the opportunity to commission a wine cup for use at the Hall, and the result is an extensive collection, expressing personal taste, that is a measure of both changing style and diversity of craftsmanship.

All these examples of plate for corporate dining are not only meant to provide the appropriate decorum for the table, but are also topics of conversation in their own right. In this they continue the tradition of the highly-fashioned and much-admired table ornaments of Renaissance princes.

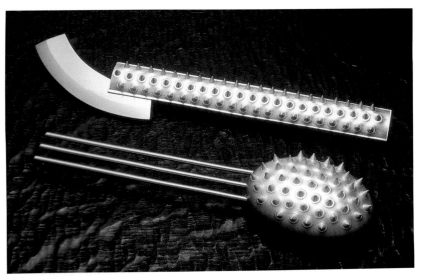

tware: cutlery
nium Canteen

ing
ing
us

Above: Table pieces commissioned from artist-craftsmen by the Silver Trust in the 1990s set out for a luncheon at the Lord Chancellor's residence.

Left: Some 15 Scottish silversmiths collaborated to create contemporary tableware for official entertaining by the First Ministers of Scotland at Bute House.

Notes on the Illustrations

All illustrations are of items in the Victoria & Albert Museum, and all photographs © Victoria & Albert Museum, unless otherwise stated

Abbreviations
NAL: National Art Library, Victoria & Albert Museum
PDP: Department of Prints, Drawings and Paintings, Victoria & Albert Museum
t = top, b = bottom, c = centre,
l = left, r = right

Jacket / Cover Soup and dinner plate: porcelain painted in underglaze blue, Chinese, made for export, *c.*1720–40 (4806L-1858, FE.14-1977). Table knife, table fork and soupspoon: silver, steel blade, London, 1738–41 (lent by N. & I. Franklin). Wine glass: lead glass, painted in enamels by William Beilby, signed 'Beilby pinxit', Newcastle-upon-Tyne, *c.*1770 (C.623-1936). Plaice dessert tureen: soft-paste porcelain painted in enamels, Chelsea, *c.*1756 (C.1451-1924). Candlesticks: silver, unmarked, after a design by George Michael Moser, London, *c.*1740 (M.329-1977). Sauceboat and salt: soft-paste porcelain painted in enamels, incised triangle marks, *c.*1745 (Schr.I.129, 2878-1901). Plates of peas and walnuts: bone china, English, possibly Mintons, *c.*1820 (Schr.I.802&A; 414:791-1885). Soup tureen and ladle: creamware, Staffordshire or Yorkshire, *c.*1790 (C.17-1945). Napkins: linen damask, Scottish, folded in the form of a fleur-de-lys (right) and German, Saxony (left), both mid-18th century (private collection). Tablecloth: linen damask, possibly Scottish, *c.*1775 (private collection). Panels: painted and gilt leather, English, *c.*1725–50 (W.14-1958)

1 See 129t; **2–3** See 28; **4tl** See 102–3; **4tr** See 132b; **4b** See 98b; **5t** See 16–17; **5b** See 82; **6** See 54

INTRODUCTION

7t Frontispiece to *A Treatise on the Use and Abuse of the Steward's Table in Families of the First Rank*, anonymous, London, 1758, engraving, Louis Philippe Boitard (by permission of the British Library)
7b Menu tablet: bone china, transfer-printed and painted in enamels, Mintons, Stoke-on-Trent, design registration mark for 23 January 1880 (Richard Dennis Publications)
8 *The Adulterous Woman Washing the Feet of Christ*: glass roundel painted in grisaille and with yellow stain, Northern Netherlands, *c.*1520–30, with surrounds of 19th-century fabrication (5634-1859)

9 Miniature buffet: pewter, English, 1580s (Museum of London)
10t Napkin folding diagrams: engraving, from Matthias Geigher, *Li Tre Trattati*, Padua, 1639 (NAL 86.U.23 p. 5)
10b *Dinner of the Order of the Bath, held in the Court of Requests, Westminster, 1725*: engraving from J. Pyne, *The Procession and Ceremonies of the Most Honourable Military Order of the Bath*, London, 1730 (Society of Antiquaries of London)
11 Detail from design for dining room decoration and furnishings: pen and ink and watercolour, Gillow & Co., English, *c.*1828 (PDP E.43-1952)
12 Trade card of Jean Henry Isenheim, Strasbourg pewterer: engraving and etching, anonymous, French, probably 1760s (National Trust, Waddesdon Manor)
13 Detail from *The Feast of Ahaseurus and Esther*: oil and tempera on oak, H. von der Heide, Lübeck, German, *c.*1500–10 (Museum für Kunst und Kulturgeschichte der Hansestadt, Lübeck)
14 Table setting: bone china designed by Peter Ting for Thomas Goode, British, 'Zen' pattern designed 1998, 'Eclipse' shape designed 1997 (courtesy of Thomas Goode and Peter Ting)
15 The I-Thai restaurant, The Hempel, London: designed by Anouska Hempel, opened 1996 (courtesy of The Hempel, London)

SETTING THE SCENE

16–17 Spice bowls: silver-gilt, engraved, mark of Roger Flynt, London, 1573–74 (M.55 to F-1946). Dishes and bowl: porcelain painted in cobalt blue, Chinese, made for export, *c.*1575–1650 (C.1461-1918, C.115-1926, C.683-1923). Bell salt with caster: silver-gilt, mark NR, London, 1594–5 (283-1893). Salt: silver-gilt, mark: a sprig, London, 1577–8 (149-1886). Goblet: soda glass, diamond-engraved with the Royal Arms of Queen Elizabeth I, attributed to Giacomo Verzellini, London, dated 1581 (C.523-1936). Beer pot: tin-glazed earthenware, Turkish, 16th century, with silver-gilt mounts, unmarked, English, *c.*1570–80 (1561-1904). Standing cups: silver-gilt, marks EW and CB in monogram, London, 1609–10 and 1616–17 (M.246-1924, M.20-1934). Pair of wedding knives: steel with handles of damascened gold set with amber, with mark of John or Joseph Jenks, with linen case embroidered in silk and silver-gilt thread, English, *c.*1600–25 (T.55-1954). Spoon with virgin and child finial, silver, parcel-gilt, London, 1577 (M.89-1952). Tablecloth: linen damask, probably by Passchier Lammertijn, Haarlem, *c.*1590,

woven with design of 'Bel and the Dragon' (private collection). Napkins: linen damask, Haarlem, *c.*1590, some folded following types in Matthias Geigher, *Li Tre Trattati*, Padua, 1639 (private collection)
18 *A Family Saying Grace*: oil on panel, Gortzius Geldorp, Flemish, 1602 (Bridgeman Art Library)
19t *A Dining Room in the Veneto*: oil on canvas, anonymous, Italian, *c.*1750 (Museo Correr, Venice)
19b *Design for the West End of the Dining Room, Kedleston, Derbyshire*: pen, ink and watercolour, with pencil, Robert Adam, 1762 (National Trust Photographic Library/ Angelo Hornak)
20 Knife box containing dinner and dessert knives and forks: mahogany veneer with silver mounts, silver flatware with mark of William Abdy, steel blades marked 'LOOKER', possibly for William Henry Looker of Leadenhall Street, London, *c.*1775 (W.65-1950)
21l *Preparations for a Tenants' Dinner in the Great Hall at Cotehele, Cornwall*: lithograph, Day and Haghe after Nicholas Condy, from Nicholas Condy, *Cotehele … the Ancient Seat of the Rt Honble Earl of Mount Edgcumbe*, *c.*1840 (NAL 100.F.17)
21r *The Dinner-Locust; or Advantages of a Keen Scent*: hand-coloured etching and aquatint, Charles Hunt after E.F. Lambert, English, *c.*1823 (collection of Simon Jervis)
22 Mermaid ewer and basin: silver-gilt, mark of TB, London, 1610–11 (M.10&A-1974). Court cupboard: carved oak, English, *c.*1600–25 (W.20-1958). Napkin: linen damask, Passchier Lammertijn, Haarlem, dated 1613 (private collection)
23t Survey drawing of the Livery Hall, Goldsmiths' Hall, London: watercolour on parchment, John Ward, English, 1692 (© The Worshipful Company of Goldsmiths)
23b *A Prospect of the Inside of Westminster Hall, shewing how the King and Queen, with the Nobility and Others did Sit at Dinner on the Day of the Coronation, 23 April 1685, with the Manner of Serving up the First Course of Hot Meat to their Majesties Table*: engraving, S. Moore, from Francis Sandford, *The History of the Coronation of the Most High, the Most might and most excellent monarch, James II …*, London, 1687 (NAL RC LL 21, p.118)
24 Design for, or drawing of, a tiered buffet for an Italian entertainment: brown ink over black chalk and watercolour, John Talman, English, *c.*1711, (PDP 29365.95)
25t Design for a sideboard: colour lithograph, from Rudolph Ackermann, *The Repository of arts, literature, commerce,*

manufactures, fashions and politics, III series, vol. 5, London, April 1825 (NAL II.RC.R.36, pl. 23, p.246)

25b Design for a sideboard for the dining hall at Dromore Castle, County Limerick, Ireland, for the 3rd Earl of Limerick: pen and wash, E. W. Godwin, English, 1869 (RIBA Library Photographs Collection)

26t *Supper at the Prince of Conti's*: oil on canvas, Michel-Barthélemy Ollivier, French, 1766 (Versailles, Musée National du Château)

26b Argand lamp: Sheffield plate, Matthew Boulton's factory, Soho, Birmingham, *c.*1815, engraved with the arms of Charles William Stewart, 1st Baron Stewart (M 14-1987)

26–7 *The Banqueting Room, the Royal Pavilion, Brighton*: coloured aquatint, J. Le Keux after A. Pugin with figures by J. Agar after J. Stephanoff, first published 1824, from *Illustrations of Her Majesty's Palace at Brighton, formerly the Pavilion ... to which is prefixed a History of the Palace by Edward Wedlake Brayley ...*, London, 1838 (NAL 100.B.32)

28 *Dinner at Haddo House*: oil on canvas, Alfred Edward Emslie, British, *c.*1884 (by courtesy of the National Portrait Gallery, London)

29t *Mariage de convenance*: oil on canvas, William Quiller Orchardson, Scottish, 1883 (Glasgow Museums: Art Gallery and Museum, Kelvingrove)

29b Design for an electric light for a dining room: pencil and watercolour on tracing paper, Nelson Ethelred Dawson, British, *c.*1904 (PDP E.738-1976)

30 Cover of *The Savoy Cocktail Book*: compiled by Harry Craddock of the Savoy Hotel, London, with decorations by Gilbert Rumbold, London, 1930 (private collection)

31t Cover illustration: Leo Fontan, *Le Sourire*, Paris, 1928 (Mary Evans Picture Library)

31c Two women downing cocktails at the bar of a chic restaurant in London's Mayfair: photograph, Felix Man, from *Picture Post*, no.80, London, 1939 (Hulton Getty)

31b Cocktail shaker: electroplate, probably designed by Keith Murray for Mappin and Webb, English, *c.*1935 (M.226-1984). Martini glass: British, 20th century (unregistered). Telescopic cigarette holder: stained wood, inlaid with silver wire, French, possibly Paris, *c.*1925 (Circ.40-1972). Cigarette case: silver with oxidized details, designed and made by Margaret Craver, London, 1946–7 (M.53-1996). Occasional table: mahogany inlaid with other woods, designed and made by Foujita, Paris, *c.*1936–8 (W.30-1979)

32 *Crayfishing*: watercolour, Carl Larsson, from the *Ett hem* series, Swedish, 1897

(Photo: National Museum of Art, Stockholm)

33t The Savoy Restaurant, Helsinki: interiors designed by Aino and Alvar Aalto, Finnish, 1937, photograph 2000 (courtesy of The Savoy Restaurant)

33b Kitchen to dining room: interior from Arthur Hald and Sven Erik Skawonius, *Contemporary Swedish Design*, Leigh-on-Sea and Stockholm, 1952 (private collection)

34 'Ruska': part of a tableware range, stoneware with mottled brown glaze, Arabia, Finnish, produced *c.*1968 (coffee pot 1986–7), designed by Ulla Procopé, 1960 (Circ.453-457-1969 and C.49&A-1988)

35l Dining area: designed by Børge Mogensen, Danish, *c.*1970–2: from *Design from Scandinavia*, no.6, 1976 (NAL)

35r Advertisement for 'Bell' stoneware: Gustavsberg tablewares designed by Karin Björquist, Swedish, 1979 (Ceramics and Glass Department archive)

36 Elizabeth David: photograph by Anthony Denney, 1960s (courtesy of the Estate of Elizabeth David)

37 Ground floor restaurant at China House, London: interior by Fusion Design and Architecture, 1999; the building was originally designed in 1919 as a showroom for the Wolseley Motor Company by William Curtis Green, who converted it to a bank in 1927 (courtesy of China House)

38t and 38bl The restaurant at the Five Arrows, Waddesdon, Buckinghamshire, with food created by James Flynn

38br Advertisement for Kenwood food mixers: American, *c.*1958 (courtesy of Kenwood Ltd)

39 The Bluebird Restaurant, London: designed by Conran & Partners, opened 1997 (courtesy of Conran Restaurants)

DRESSING THE TABLE

40–41 Soup tureens: painted in enamels and gilt, some enamelling by J.H. O'Neale, gold anchor mark (tureens) and red anchor (stands), *c.*1758 (C.222-1935 & C.680-1925, C.221-1935). Two soup plates: painted in underglaze blue, *c.*1755 (2965-1901, Schr.I.128). Two dinner plates: painted in enamels, red anchor mark, *c.*1753–5 (C.119&A-1980). Salts and sauceboats, painted in enamels, incised triangle marks (C.171-1940, 2878-1901, Schr.I.129&A). *All the above are of Chelsea soft-paste porcelain.* Two soup plates and dinner plates: porcelain painted in underglaze blue, Chinese, *c.*1720–40, made for export (4806L-1858, C.1356-1924, FE.13, 14-1977). Soup ladle: silver, unidentified mark WW, London, 1764–5 (Circ.488-1921). Candlesticks: silver, unmarked, after a design by George Michael

Moser, London, *c.*1740 (M.329-1977). Table knives, table forks and soup spoons: silver with steel blades, various sponsors' marks, London, 1738–41 (lent by N. & I. Franklin). Tablecloth: linen damask, possibly Scottish, *c.*1775 (private collection). Napkins: linen damask, German, Saxony, *c.*1765, all with English 18th-century provenances, folded as the napkins at the Coronation of the King of the Romans, Frankfurt, 1763 (private collection). Panels: painted and gilt leather, English, *c.*1725–50 (W.14-1958)

42l Trencher: beech, English, 16th or 17th century (Crown copyright: Historic Royal Palaces. Reproduced by permission of Historic Royal Palaces under licence from the Controller of Her Majesty's Stationery Office)

42r Trencher salt: silver-gilt, mark RA with a quatrefoil below, London, 1629–30, engraved 'Iohn Lane Vintner at ye mermaide neare Chearing crosse' (Worshipful Company of Vintners)

43t Set of roundels: probably beech, faced with hand-coloured woodcuts, English, *c.*1600–30 (401-1878)

43b Porringer: tin-glazed earthenware splashed with cobalt and manganese, London, late 17th or early 18th century (Museum of London)

44 'Pan' wall-bracket: gilt-wood, English, *c.*1760, from Langley Park, Norfolk, and similar to a design in Thomas Chippendale, *Gentleman and Cabinet-Maker's Director*, 3rd edition, London, 1763 (W.50-1946)

45t Silver wine-cooler: engraving, Gerard Scotin II after Hubert Gravelot, English, 1735; the cooler was commissioned in 1730 by Littleton Poyntz Meynell through the goldsmith-banker Henry Jernegan; it was designed under his direction by George Vertue; models were supplied by Michael Rysbrack, and the cistern bears marks for Charles Kandler, London, 1734 (PDP E.1594-1948)

45b Pattern for a sideboard-table or 'Frame for marble slab': engraving, Matthew Darly, from Thomas Chippendale, *Gentleman and Cabinet-Maker's Director*, 3rd edition, London, 1763 (NAL RC.CC.13, pl.CLXXVI)

46l Mirror (girandole): gilt-wood with brass candle-nozzles, Thomas Chippendale, English, *c.*1766, commissioned by the Duke of Portland and invoiced in 1766 (2388-1855)

46r Candle stand: painted wood with brass candle-nozzles, English, *c.*1758, commissioned by George Lyttelton, 1st Lord Lyttelton, for the gallery at Hagley Hall, Worcestershire, and similar to a design in Thomas Johnson, *Collection of Designs*, London, 1758 (W.9-1950)

47 The 'Newdigate' Centrepiece: silver, mark of Paul de Lamerie, London, 1743–4; commissioned in 1743 by the Rt Hon. Sophia, Baroness Lempster to celebrate the marriage of her granddaughter Sophia Conyers and Sir Richard Newdigate, 5th Baronet (M.149-1919)

48l *Le Superbe Repas Presenté au Roy et aux Princes de sa Cour, 1729*: engraving, from *Almanach royal*, Paris, 1730 (Bibliothèque nationale de France, Paris, Département des Estampes)

48r *A Table of Fifteen or Sixteen Covers*: engraving, from Vincent La Chapelle, *The Modern Cook*, 2nd edition, London, 1736 (The Blanche Leigh Collection, Brotherton Library, University of Leeds)

49 *The Dining Room*: watercolour, Mary Ellen Best, English, *c.*1838 (Bridgeman Art Library)

50–51 Dining table with floral decorations: lithograph, frontispiece to Mrs Isabella Beeton, *The Book of Household Management*, London, 1888 (private collection)

51t *The Dinner Party*: wood engraving, signed 'Roberts', British, 1890 (Mansell Collection)

51b Parlourmaid and underparlourmaid ready to serve dinner: photograph, Bill Brandt, British, 1933 (PDP Ph.17-1978, © Bill Brandt/Bill Brandt Archive Ltd)

52 Napkin: linen damask, Dutch, mid-17th century, woven with view of London and the inscription 'LONDINIUM BRITANNIA METROPOLIS ET EMPORIUM' (T.39-1982)

53t Part of a tablecloth: linen damask, Flemish, *c.*1630, woven with the story of Tamar, Amnon and Absalon (T.145-1929)

53b Napkin: linen damask, German, *c.*1710, woven with bizarre silk pattern (T.451-1970)

54 Travelling set of cutlery: silver-gilt, mark TT below a coronet, London, *c.*1690 (M.62-C-1949)

55t Dessert knife and fork: soft-paste porcelain handle painted in underglaze blue, French, probably St Cloud, steel blade, English, *c.*1720 (courtesy of Bill Brown). 'Merryman' plate: tin-glazed earthenware painted in cobalt blue, English, 1727 (private collection). Wineglass: lead glass, English, *c.*1715, inscribed 'GOD SAVE KING GEORGE' (C.135-1925). Napkin: linen damask, German, early 18th century, inscribed 'STAD ANTWERPEN' and 'DER HERZOG VON MARLBORUK' (T.454-1970)

55b Table knife and fork: green ivory handles and silver ferrules, steel blade and tines, English, *c.*1760–80 (courtesy of Bill Brown). Plate: creamware painted and transfer-printed in enamels, Wedgwood's factory, Etruria, *c.*1771–5, transfer-printed in

Liverpool by Guy Green with 'The Tiger and the Fox' from *Aesop's Fables* (Schr.II.401D). Wineglass: lead glass, English, *c.*1773, engraved 'Mary Jones 1773' (C.15-1976). Tablecloth: linen damask, German, mid-18th century (T.62-1929)

56t Trade card of Henry Patten, razor maker and cutler: engraving and etching, Edward Warner, London, *c.*1750 (E.571-1946)

56b Ice spade, mark of William Eley I and William Fearn, London, 1800–1 (anonymous loan). Pudding trowel: silver, mark of Richard Meach, London, 1774–5 (M.306-1962). Fish slice: silver, the blade with mark of William Eley I and William Fearn, the handle with unidentified mark IT, London, 1800–1 (M.101-1916)

57 Set of manufacturer's patterns for flatware: teaspoon, dessert fork, dessert spoon, table spoon, table knife and dessert knife (?), silver and silver-gilt with steel blades, mark of John S. Hunt, London, 1850, blades with mark of Hunt and Roskell, 'Lord Harris' pattern (M.65, M.66-1966)

58t Design for, or drawing of, a display for an Italian entertainment: brown ink and watercolour over black chalk, John Talman, English, *c.*1711 (PDP 29365.96)

58b Table plan showing floral arrangement for a breakfast table: colour lithograph, from John Perkins, *Floral Designs …*, London, 1877 (NAL 101.A.31, pl.3)

59t Reconstruction of a banquet held by Christian VII of Denmark at Christiansborg Palace, Denmark, in 1770; reconstructed in 1988 in the dining room of his palace at Amalienborg (The Royal Silver Room, Copenhagen)

59b Private Supper at The Savoy Hotel, London: photograph, Bedford Lemere, British, 1895 (© English Heritage NMR)

60 Silversmith's drawing of condiment vases and stands: pen and ink and grey wash, English, probably London, *c.*1785–90 (PDP 8389.14)

61t Tureen and underdish (*pot à oglio* or *pot à oille*): hard-paste porcelain painted in enamels and gilt, Sèvres, 1777 (a shape first made at Vincennes, *c.*1752–3) (C.28-1922)

61b Pair of sauce tureens and stands: silver, mark of Benjamin Smith, London, 1807–8; made to match the soup tureens designed for Lord Mountford by William Kent and made by George Wickes in 1744; the design was published in John Vardy, *Some Designs of Mr. Inigo Jones and Mr. Wm. Kent*, London, 1744 (private collection; photograph © Bruce White 2001)

62 Cruet frame: silver-gilt with cut-glass bottles, mark of John Scofield, London,

1793–4 (Lonsdale loan 125)

63t Pair of pepper pots: silver and enamel, mark of Cohen and Charles, London, 1900 (courtesy of Brian Beet)

63b Sugar caster: silver, mark of Walker and Hall, Sheffield, 1932–3 (anonymous loan to Bristol City Museum and Art Gallery)

64 The Vyvyan Salt: silver-gilt with panels of painted glass, mark WH over a flower in a plain shield, London, 1592–3 (M.273-1925)

65t 'L'Hyver' ('Winter', from a set of the Four Seasons): engraving, Abraham Bosse, French, *c.*1630–40 (Trustees of the British Museum)

65b The Moody Salt: silver, mark WH, probably for Wolfgang Howzer, London, 1664–5 (M.347-1912)

66t Epergne: silver with cut glass bowls, mark of Thomas Pitts, London, 1764–5 (M.1703-1944)

66b Design for a 'surtout': woodcut from François Massialot, *Le nouveau Cuisiner Royal et Bourgeois*, Paris, 1716 edition (NAL)

67 Centrepiece with caster and cruets: hard-paste porcelain painted in enamels and gilt, Meissen, *c.*1755–60 (C.88-1918)

68 Dish cover: silvered brass, English, *c.*1732, engraved with the crest of Charles Howard, 3rd Earl Carlisle (M.38-1994)

69t Dish-warmer: Sheffield plate with bone handles and ebony feet, English, *c.*1810 (M.354-1922). Argyle: silver, mark of T. Phipps and E. Robinson, London, 1808–9 (M.55-1982). Hot-water plate: porcelain painted in enamels, Chinese, *c.*1750, made for the European market (2912-1901)

69b Extendable dish cross: engraving with manuscript annotations, from a Sheffield plate manufacturer's catalogue, attributed to Matthew Boulton, English, *c.*1780 (PDP E.639-1927, fol.65r)

70–71 Detail from a cross section of the Royal Pavilion, Brighton, showing the Great Kitchen and Banqueting Room: coloured aquatint, first published 1824, from *Illustrations of Her Majesty's Palace at Brighton, formerly the Pavilion … to which is prefixed a History of the Palace by Edward Wedlake Brayley …*, London, 1838 (NAL 100.B.32)

71l Plate-warmer: gunmetal and ormolu on parcel-gilt mahogany base, Diedrich Nicholaus Anderson, London, 1760, from Kedleston, Derbyshire (National Trust Photographic Library/Nadia MacKenzie)

71b Frontispiece to H.M. Kinsley, *One Hundred Recipes for the Chafing Dish*, Gorham Manufacturing Company, New York, 1894 (NAL 500.A.156)

72t *A Midnight Modern Conversation*: engraving, printed in red, William Hogarth,

English, 1732/3 (PDP F.118 (93))

72b *A Voluptuary under the horrors of Digestion*: hand-coloured etching, James Gillray, English, 1792 (PDP 2376)

73 *Hero'es Recruiting at Kelsey's*: hand-coloured etching, James Gillray, English, 1797 (PDP 28900.C.1)

74t *'L'Après dinee des Anglais, Par un français prisonnier de Guerre'*: hand-coloured engraving, anonymous, published Paris, c.1814 (Trustees of the British Museum)

74b *Night and Morning*: hand-coloured etchings, 'Shortshanks' (pseudonym for Robert Seymour), English, c.1830 (PDP E.982-1970)

75 *Mr Burwin-Fosselton at supper*: pen and ink, Walter Weedon Grossmith, c.1888, illustration to George and Walter Weedon Grossmith, *The Diary of a Nobody*, London, 1888–92 (PDP E.629-1987)

76 Still life: oil on panel, Godfried van Wedig, German, early 17th century (private collection; photograph courtesy of the art dealers Hoogsteder and Hoogsteder, The Hague, the Netherlands)

77t Detail from *The Wedding at Cana*: oil on canvas, Paolo Veronese, Venetian, 1563 (Louvre, Paris, © Photo RMN)

77b Design for an elaborate wineglass: pen and ink and wash, Jacobo Ligozzi, Florentine, 1617 (Gabinetto Disegnie e Stampe, Uffizi, Florence)

78 *Tazza*: with applied *lattimo* thread and gilding, Netherlands or Venice, c.1550–1600 (C.2463-1910). Goblet: with tooled stem and diamond-engraved bowl, probably Netherlands, 17th century, inscribed '*In Vino Veritas*' (C.138-1956). Flute glass: with gilding, Netherlands, c.1575–1625 (1811-1855). *Roemer* (wineglass): green glass with applied prunts, Germany or Netherlands, c.1625–75 (C.288-1936). Goblet and cover: with tooled decoration, Netherlands or Venice, 17th century (580&A-1903)

79t Tankard, possibly for beer: filigree glass ('*a fili*') with applied and moulded decoration and gilding and pewter mount and cover, probably southern Netherlands, c.1575–1650 (587-1903). *Passglas* (beaker): green glass with trailed threads, Netherlands, c.1580–1650 (C.37-1958). Beaker: diamond engraved, signed by Willem Mooleyser of Rotterdam, northern Netherlands, 1685 (C.431-1936). Beaker: ice glass with applied and moulded decoration and gilding, Netherlands, 17th century (408-1854). Beaker: filigree glass ('*a fili*'), northern Netherlands, possibly Amsterdam, c.1600–50 (1864-1855).

79b Goblet: lead glass, inscribed 'God Bless Queen Ann', English, early 18th century

(C.539-1936). Wine glass: lead glass, English, c.1700–20 (C.115-1925).

THE DESSERT

80–81 A recreation of a dessert setting in the 1880 dining room at Waddesdon Manor, Buckinghamshire. Part-dessert service: soft-paste porcelain painted in enamels and gilt, Sèvres, 1766, made for Louis-César-Renaud, Vicomte de Choiseul, shown with plateau set with Sèvres biscuit porcelain figures and vases together with sugar and coloured sand parterre (The Country Life Picture Library)

82 Spice bowl: silver-gilt, engraved with 'Abram sacrificing Isaac', mark of Roger Flynt, London, 1573-4 (M.55-1946)

82–3 *Still life with the Poor Man and the Rich Lazarus*: oil on panel, Osias Beert I, Flemish, early 17th century (photograph courtesy of the art dealers Hoogsteder and Hoogsteder, The Hague, the Netherlands)

83b Dish: silver, mark of F with C or G, London, 1618–19 (M.11-1932). Knife: steel with silver mounts and jasper handle, mark of Joseph Strutt, London, c.1640 (M.42-1954). Wineglass: Venice, 17th century (5227-1859). Napkin: linen damask, Haarlem, early 17th century, woven with design of the 'Tree of Jesse' (private collection)

84 Sweetmeat glass: cut and painted in black enamel, Bohemia, c.1730, enamelled in the style of Ignaz Preissler (C.227-1922). *Tazza*: glass with traces of gilding, and diamond-point engraving, Venice, 16th–17th century, inscribed 'S. ALFONS. GLARA … CAP DE. JUSTIA' (C.215-1936)

85t Detail from *The Sense of Taste*: oil on canvas, Philippe Mercier, c.1743-6 (photograph by courtesy of Sotheby's)

85b Sucket fork: iron, parcel-gilt, French, c.1550, from a travelling set comprising knife, fork, skewer and leather case (M.602-1910)

86l An ice-cellar: engraving, from Robert Boyle, *New Experiments and Observations touching Cold …*, London, 1683 (By permission of the British Library)

86r Drawing of a French porcelain ice-cream pail (*seau à glace*): pencil, pen and ink and watercolour, from the *Original Drawing Book No. 1* of the Leeds creamware manufacturers Hartley and Green, probably 1790s (E.576-1941, p. 94)

87 *Seau à glace, tasses à glaces, plateau Bouret* and *seau à bouteille* (with modern bottle), soft-paste porcelain painted in enamels and gilt, Sèvres, c.1766, from the service presented to Prince Starhemberg by Louis XV in 1766 (National Trust, Waddesdon Manor)

88 *Seau à glace* from The Egyptian Service: hard-paste porcelain painted in enamels and

gilt, Sèvres, 1811, probably designed by Alexandre Brachard, the decoration after engravings by Vivant Denon; the service was originally ordered for the Empress Josephine in 1809–10 and presented to the Duke of Wellington in 1818 (C.128-1979)

89t Ice-cream pail: cut glass, Perrin Geddes & Co., Warrington, c.1810 (C.211-1931). Piggins and custard or lemonade cups: cut and moulded, English, 1810–30 (Circ.407-1912, Circ.357-1965, C.300E-1976, C.178-1923)

89b *John Bull and his family at an Ice Café*: lithograph, J.J. Chalon, English, c.1820 (courtesy of Robin Weir)

90t Left to right. Dessert plate: soft-paste porcelain painted in enamels and gilt, Derby, c.1773, from a service supplied to Philip Egerton of Oulton, Cheshire, in 1773 (C.23-1978). Plate: hard-paste porcelain painted in enamels and gilt, Meissen, c.1737, modelled by J.J. Kändler from the Swan Service commissioned by Count Brühl in 1737 (C.6-1956). Dessert plate: soft-paste porcelain painted in enamels and gilt, Sèvres, 1778, painted by Vincent Taillandier, from a service commissioned by Catherine II of Russia (C.449-1921)

90b Sugar tureen: soft-paste porcelain painted in enamels, Chantilly, French, c.1735–50 (161-1887)

91 Part-dessert service: soft-paste porcelain painted in enamels and gilt, Sèvres, 1766; made for Louis-Cèsar-Renaud, Vicomte de Choiseul (© Christie's Images Ltd 2000)

92t Sugar sculptures representing moral virtues: engraving, Arnold van Westerhout after Giovanni Battista Lenardi, the sculptures attributed to Cirro Ferri, from John Michael Wright, *An Account of His Excellence Roger Earl of Castlemaine's Embassy*, London, 1688 (NAL 12 (3) pl.13)

92b Design for a plateau with figures, sweetmeat glasses and parterre: engraving, from Joseph Gilliers, *Le Cannameliste Français*, Nancy, 1751 (NAL 20K pl.5)

93 Figure group of a gallant and a lady watched by a man: hard-paste porcelain painted in enamels and gilt, Meissen, c.1750-5, modelled by J.J. Kändler (C.145-1931, C.50-1962)

94 '*Ruine de Palmire*': design for a confectionery centrepiece, lithograph, signed 'Thierry', from Marie Antonin Carême, *La patissier pittoresque*, 3rd edition, Paris, 1828 (NAL 35.E.17, pl.53)

95t Centrepiece from The Egyptian Service: biscuit hard-paste porcelain, Sèvres, 1810–12, designed by Jean-Baptiste Le Peyre (or Lepère) after engravings after Vivant Denon; the service was originally ordered for the Empress Josephine in 1809–10 and presented to the Duke of Wellington in 1818 (C.132-1979)

95b Figure of a bride as Europa with 10 attendants: hard-paste porcelain painted in underglaze colours and gilt, Royal Porcelain Factory (K.P.M.), Berlin, 1913–18, designed by Adolf Amberg in 1904, first made as a table setting for the wedding of the German Crown Prince in 1905 (C.84-E-1987, C.175-C-1986)

96 Wine fountain, cistern and cooler: silver, mark of Anthony Nelme, London, 1719–20, made for Thomas Parker, later 1st Earl of Macclesfield (M.25-27-1998)

97 '*Un dîner dans la salle des fêtes au palais des princes de Salm*': oil on canvas, anonymous, French, *c.*1770 (collection des tableaux du salon d'honneur de l'Hôtel de Ville de Raon-l'Etape; photo: Gilbert Magnin)

98t 'Jolly boat': Sheffield plate, English, *c.*1800 (M.630-1936). Decanter: cut-glass, English, *c.*1800–10 (Circ.138, 139-1938)

98b Decanter: glass with silver mounts, the finial set with chrysoprase, mark of The Guild of Handicraft, London, 1904–5, designed by C.R. Ashbee (M.121-1966)

99t Bottle tickets. Port: silver, unmarked, English, early 19th century. Hock: mother-of-pearl, English, mid-18th century. White: silver, mark of Hester Bateman, London, *c.*1780. Madeira: silver-gilt, mark of Digby Scott and Benjamin Smith, London, 1806–7. Sherry: silver, mark of RH, London, 1877–8. Cyder: ivory, English, early 19th century. Sloe Gin: painted enamels on copper, English, *c.*1770 (M.1117, M.1458-, M.490-, M.904-, M.37-, M.1374-, M.1514-1944)

99b Monteith: silver, mark of Joseph Ward, London, 1709–10 (M.14-1973). Wine glasses: lead glass, English, early 18th century, one with knop enclosing a silver coin of 1701 (C.538-1936, C.135-1925)

100–1 Ceramic tureens and plates with trompe l'oeil decoration, all painted in enamels. Melon, cauliflower, asparagus, and plaice dessert tureens, and chicken soup tureen: soft-paste porcelain, Chelsea, *c.*1756 (2938-1901, C.52-1968, C.176-1940, C.1451-1924, C.1995-1940). Butter pot (?) with pike finial: tin-glazed earthenware, Delft, *c.*1770 (2945-1853). Purple cabbage: tin-glazed earthenware, probably German, mid-18th century (C.164-1912). Trick plate (*plato de engany*) with peppers: tin-glazed earthenware, Alcora, Spain, *c.*1764–84 (333-1876). Green cabbage: porcelain, English, probably 1820s (C.33-1944). Plates of peas and walnuts: bone china, English, possibly Mintons, Stoke-on-Trent, *c.*1820 (Schr.I.802&A; 414:791-1885)

AFTER DINNER

102–3 Wine glass: clear glass, James Powell & Sons, Whitefriars, London, designed by Philip Webb for Morris, Marshall, Faulkner & Co., possibly *c.*1862–3 (C.81-1959). Decanter: green glass, James Powell & Sons, Whitefriars, London, designed by T.G. Jackson, *c.*1870 (Circ.155-1959). Wine bottle: green glass, labelled 'Imperial Tokay Dry Grande Reserve, 1864' (private collection). Candlesticks: copper, English, 1861–3, designed by Philip Webb for Morris, Marshall, Faulkner & Co. (M.1130-1926). Bowl: lead-glazed earthenware with slip decoration, Mannheim, Germany, *c.*1850–75 (C.228-1926). Table: oak, George Myers, English, *c.*1854, designed by George Edmund Street (W.88-1975). Armchair: ebonized beech with rush seat, Morris & Co., English, *c.*1870–90, possibly designed by Philip Webb and first made by Morris, Marshall, Faulkner & Co., *c.*1860. Interior: the Green Dining Room at the Victoria & Albert Museum: decorated by Morris, Marshall, Faulkner & Co., 1866–8.

104 *Humpen* (beer glass): glass, painted in enamels with a miner and his wife, German, probably Franconia, 1671 (95-1853)

105t Wassail set and table: lignum vitae and ebony with ivory, English, *c.*1640–80, from Rushden Hall, Northamptonshire (W.8-1976)

105b Tyg: lead glazed earthenware with slip decoration, Wrotham, English, 1649 (C.118-1938). Tyg or Wassail bowl: lead glazed earthenware, Wiltshire, 1702 (C.35-1987). Tyg: lead glazed earthenware with slip decoration, Staffordshire, 1710, inscribed 'TOMAS DAKIN MADE TIS CUP FOR MARY SCULLTHARP OR HER FRIEND AB 1710' (C.770-1922)

106 Punch bowl: hard-paste porcelain painted in enamels with ormolu stand, Meissen, *c.*1750–70; the punch-drinking scene is copied from William Hogarth's *Midnight Modern Conversation* (C.37 &A-1960)

107t Wine glass: lead glass, painted in enamels, English, *c.*1759, inscribed 'Success to the British Fleet' C.175-1925). Glass: lead glass with air-twist stem and engraved decoration, English, *c.*1755–60, inscribed 'King of Prussia' (C.194-1925). Election glass: lead glass, Newcastle-upon-Tyne, *c.*1770, probably enamelled by William Beilby, inscribed 'Liberty & Clavering For Ever' (C.632-1936). 10-pint tankard: salt-glazed stoneware, and marked 'John Harwell', Bristol, 1739, inscribed 'Southwell for Ever JH WCM 1739' (Schr.II.62; 414:855-1885). Firing glass: lead glass, English, *c.*1820–40, engraved with motto and cypher of the Duke of Sussex (C.652-1936).

Decanter: lead glass, English, *c.*1761, engraved 'LOWTHER AND UPTON HUZZA', referring to the Westmorland parliamentary election of 1761 (C.322-1931). Wine and water glass: lead glass with air-twist stem, English, mid-18th century, engraved 'Rede' and 'Fiat' and with Jacobite emblems (C.136-1937).

107b *The Toast*: etching and aquatint, drawn and etched by Henry Alken, aquatint by G. Hunt, English, 1824 (NAL)

108t Eight tiles from a trade sign: tin-glazed earthenware painted in colours, London, early 18th century (Museum of London)

108b Tea tray: tin-glazed earthenware painted in cobalt blue, English, probably London, 1743 (3864-1901)

109 *Le Dejeuner de Famille*: pastel, Jean-Etienne Liotard, 1750 (private collection)

110t Tray and teapot from a déjeuner (cabaret set): tin-glazed earthenware, Niderviller, France, the tray dated 1774, painted in enamels by J. Deutsch, (481-1870, C.251-1951)

110b Coffee pot (*Cafetière éléphant*): porcelain with *pâte-sur-pâte* decoration and gilding, Sèvres, *c.*1762, designed by Marc Louis Emmanuel Solon, shown at the International Exhibition, London, 1862 (8055-1862)

111 Coffee service: silver with ivory plugs, designed and made by W.G. Sissons, Sheffield, 1872–3 (Circ.97-100-1961). Tea tray: electroplate, engraved, with cast and applied handles, Elkington & Co., Birmingham, 1885 (M.244-1984). Cup and saucer: bone china painted in enamels and gilt, Mintons, Stoke-on-Trent, also with mark of A.B. Daniell & Son, Wigmore Street, London, shown at the Centennial Exhibition, Philadelphia, 1875 (574-1877)

112t *A Game of Whist*: coloured etching and aquatint, I. R. and G. Cruikshank, from Pierce Egan, *Life in London*, London, 1821 (NAL G.28.C.15)

112b *Lady Godina's Rout – or – Peeping Tom spying out Pope-Joan*: hand-coloured etching, James Gillray, English, 1796 (PDP 1232(82)-1882)

113t *The Passenger to Boulogne*: engraving, from Professor G. Hoffmann, *Drawing Room Amusements*, London, 1879 (G.29.Y.61, p. 140)

113b *The Rake at the Gaming Tables*: book illustration, David Low, from Rebecca West, *The Modern Rake's Progress*, London, 1934 (NAL 501.C.41)

CELEBRATIONS AND CEREMONIES

114–15 Centrepiece, plateau, soup tureens, covered dishes, dinner plates, soup plates, soup ladle, and knives, forks and spoons from the Portuguese Service: silver, parcel-gilt, Lisbon, 1812–16, designed by Domingos Antonio de Sequiera; salt cellars, silver-gilt, mark of Robert Garrard, London, 1819–20 (WM.745-1948)

116 A dinner at Fontainbleau (*'Disposition du Festin fait par Sa Majesté a Messierus les Chevaliers après leurs Creations faite à Fontain Blau le 14 May 1633'*): engraving, Abraham Bosse, French, 1733 (Trustees of the British Museum)

117t *Charles I, Queen Henrietta Maria and Charles, Prince of Wales, Dining in Public*: oil on panel, Gerrit Houckgeest, 1635 (Royal Collection © 2001, Her Majesty the Queen)

117b *A Ground Plott of Westminster Hall [showing] … The Manner of placing the Mets on their Majesties Table … [on the Day of their Coronation, 23 April 1685]*: etching, from Francis Sandford, *The History of the Coronation of the Most High, the Most might and most excellent monarch, James II …*, London, 1687 (NAL RC LL 21)

118t *Regency Fete: or John Bull in the Conservatory*: hand-coloured etching, Charles Williams ('Argus'), English, 1811 (Trustees of the British Museum)

118b *The Gothic Dining Room at Carlton House, London*: hand-coloured aquatint, T. Sutherland after C. Wild, 1817, from W. H. Pyne, *The History of the Royal Residences …*, London, 1819 (NAL RC.LL.72 p.63)

119 The dining room at Sandringham House, Norfolk: photograph, Bedford Lemere, British, 1890s (PDP, 109-1926)

120t Christmas card: hand-coloured lithograph, designed by Sir Henry Cole and John Calcott Horsley, English, 1843 (PDP E.687-1913)

120b Christmas pudding plate: earthenware, printed and painted in enamels, Staffordshire, possibly Copeland, *c*.1850 (Richard Dennis Publications)

121t 'May Christmas be thy harbinger of joy!': Christmas card, colour lithograph, anonymous, British, *c*.1870 (private collection)

121b *Daisy and I survey the Xmas dinner. Prospects of a good time*: watercolour and gouache, Charlie Hammond, English, *c*.1880, from Christopher Fry, *Charlie Hammond's Sketch-Book*, Oxford, 1980 (© 1980, reproduced by permission of Oxford University Press)

122 *An Allegory of True Love*: oil on panel, Pieter Pourbus, Flemish, *c*.1547 (reproduced by permission of the Wallace Collection, London)

123t *Feast in honour of the birth of the Dauphin, first son of Louis XV*: watercolour, anonymous, French, 1729 (Bibliothèque municipale, Lille)

123b *The Picnic (Epping Forest)*: colour lithograph, anonymous, British, *c*.1880–90, from a set of trade cards issued by the biscuit manufacturers Huntley and Palmers (PDP E.1822-1983)

124 Bill from *Au Gourmand*, Paris: etching and engraving with manuscript bill, anonymous, French, 1808 (National Trust, Waddesdon Manor)

125t *A dining car on the Great Northern Railway*: engraving, anonymous, from *The Illustrated London News*, 22 November 1879 (NAL PP 10)

125b *Two boys of Athelstan were dining together at a cheap Italian restaurant in Soho*: pencil, bodycolour and wash on board, Amédée Forestier, 1900, original drawing for illustration to Walter Besant, *The Five Year's Tryst* in *The Illustrated London News*, 1900 (PDP E.4100-1914)

126–7 *The Waterloo Banquet of 1836*: oil on canvas, William Salter, English, 1840 (By kind permission of His Grace the Duke of Wellington)

126b *The Waterloo Gallery*: watercolour, Joseph Nash, English, 1852 (WM.1-1981)

128 Obelisk with river gods: hard paste porcelain painted in enamels and gilt, Berlin, 1817–19, figures designed in workshop of Johann Gottfried Schadow; mount of gilded bronze made by Salpuis; the central section of the centrepiece from the Prussian Service presented to the Duke of Wellington in 1819 (WM.940-, WM.975-982-1948)

129t Oval soup tureen: silver, parcel-gilt, Lisbon, 1814, designed by Domingos Antonio de Sequiera, decorated with the arms of the Duque da Victoria, signed *D. A. Sequiera Lusitano a fez em Lisboa 1814*; from the Portuguese Service presented to the Duke of Wellington in 1816 (WM.733-1948)

129bl Dessert plate: hard-paste porcelain painted in enamels and gilt, Meissen, 1818–20, painted with a view of Apsley House, from the Saxon Service presented to the Duke of Wellington in 1820 (WM.1119-1948)

129br One of a pair of sucriers: hard-paste porcelain painted in enamels and gilt, Sèvres, designed by Jean-Charles-Nicholas Brachard and gilt by Micaud; from the Egyptian Service ordered by Empress Josephine in 1810 but rejected by her and presented to the Duke of Wellington by Louis XVIII in 1818. (C.127-1979)

130l The Ritz Restaurant, London: photograph, 1906 (© English Heritage. NMR)

130r *Supper after the Show at the Ritz*: illustration by Dorothea St. John George, from Horace Wyndham, *Nights in London. Where Mayfair Makes Merry*, London, 1926

(Museum of London)

131l The Ritz Restaurant, London: photograph by James Mortimer, late 1990s (courtesy of The Ritz, London)

131r Menu from The Ritz Restaurant, 2000 (courtesy of The Ritz, London)

132a Setting for dessert in the panelled room of the Senior Common Room at New College, Oxford (courtesy of the Warden and Fellows of New College, Oxford; photo Victoria and Albert Museum)

132b Court of Assistants' Lunch in the Luncheon Room at Goldsmiths' Hall, London, 2001 (photograph © The Worshipful Company of Goldsmiths, photographer Clarissa Bruce)

133 St George Centrepiece, Downing Street Commission: silver, parcel-gilt with patinations and mosaic work set with lapis lazuli, mother-of-pearl, coral, ebony and amber, Kevin Coates, London, 1993 (courtesy of the Silver Trust)

134 37D Table knife and combined spoon and fork: silver, Chris Knight, 1991, for the Sheffield Millennium Canteen (courtesy of Sheffield City Council and the Association of British Designer Silversmiths)

135t Luncheon table laid out in the River Room at the Lord Chancellor's residence, House of Lords, 1999, showing some of the Silver Trust pieces in use. These include: water jug by Keith Redfern, fruit bowl by Toby Russell, cruets set with cabochon lapis lazuli with matching pepperettes by Richard Fox, candelabra by Michael Rowe and made up by Norman Bassant, engraved beakers by Gerald Benney, fruit stands with lion and unicorn bases by Lexi Dick, chased flower bowl by Rod Kelly, octagonal flower bowl by Michael Lloyd, butter dishes by Martin Pugh, and underplate designed by Lawrence Blackwell and engraved by Ray Wilkins (photograph by Alf Barnes courtesy of the Silver Trust)

135b The Millenium Collection for Bute House: comprising silver by Malcolm Appleby (table-centre), Gordon Burnett (clock), John Creed (candleholders), Maureen Edgar (condiment set), Adrian Hope (cutlery), Marion Kane (vases), William Kirk (rose/fruit bowl), Michael Lloyd (water jugs), Grant McCaig (fruit bowl), Helen Marriot (candlesticks), Roger Millar (wine cooler), Graham Stewart (claret jugs), Sarah Cave (condiment set), Linda Robertson (condiment set), and Nicola Williams (feature bowl and candlesticks), Edinburgh, 2000–1 (The Incorporation of Goldsmiths of the City of Edinburgh; Shannon Tofts Photography © 2001)

Selected Further Reading

Belden, L.C., *The Festive Tradition: Table Decoration and Desserts in America, 1650–1900*, London and New York, 1983

Binney, M., *The Ritz Hotel*, London, 1999

Black, M., *Food and Cooking in 19th-Century Britain*, London, 1985

Blacker, M.R., *Flora domestica: A History of Flower Arranging, 1500–1930*, London, 2000

Brears, P., *Food and Cooking in 16th-Century Britain*, London, 1985

Brears, P., *Food and Cooking in 17th-Century Britain*, London, 1985

Brett, G., *Dinner is Served: A History of Dining in England, 1400–1900*, London, 1968

British Museum, *Catalogue of Personal and Political Satires*, 11 vols, London, 1870–1954

Brown, P., *In Praise of Hot Liquors*, Fairfax House, York, 1995

Brown, P. (ed.), *British Cutlery: A History of its Design, Evolution and Use*, London, 2001

Brown, P. and Day, I., *Pleasures of the Table*, Fairfax House, York, 1997

Brown, P. and Schwarz, M.H., *Come Drink the Bowl Dry*, Fairfax House, York, 1996

Burgers, C.A., 'Some Notes on Western European Table Linen from the 16th through the 18th Centuries' in Cooke, E.S. (ed.), *Upholstery in America and Europe: From the 17th Century to World War I*, New York, 1987

Bursche, S., *Tafelzier des Barock*, Munich, 1974

Catterall, C. (ed.), *Food: Design and Culture*, London and Glasgow, 1999

Charleston, R.J., 'A Background to the Earliest English Porcelain Figures', *Antiques Review* I (June/August 1951), pp.23–8

Charleston, R.J., *English Glass and the Glass used in England, c.400–1940*, London, 1984

Charleston, R.J., 'Glasses for the Dessert I: Introductory', *The Glass Circle*, no.5, 1986, pp.27–32

David, E., *A Book of Mediterranean Food*, London, 1950

David, E., *An Omelette and a Glass of Wine*, London, 1984

Day, I. (ed.), *Eat, Drink and Be Merry: The British at Table, 1600–2000*, London, 2000

de Bellaigue, G., 'A Royal Mise-en-Scène: George IV's Coronation Banquet', *Furniture History*, xxix (1993), pp.174–83

Emmerson, R., *British Teapots and Tea Drinking*, London, 1992

Emmerson, R., *Table Settings*, Harverfordwest, 1991

Khachadourian, S., *The Cocktail Shaker: The Tanqueray Guide*, London, 2000

Elias, N., *The Civilizing Process*, Oxford, 1994

Ennès, P., Mabille, G., and Thiébaut, *Histoire de la Table*, Paris, 1994

Feild, R., *Irons in the Fire: A History of Cooking Equipment*, Marlborough, 1984

Glanville, P., *Silver in England*, 1987

Glanville, P., *Silver in Tudor and Early Stuart England*, 1989

Glanville, P. (ed.), *Silver*, 1996

Hardyment, C., *Slice of Life: The British Way of Eating Since 1945*, London, 1997

Hughes, G. B., 'Keeping Georgian Food Hot', *Country Life*, 144, December 1968, pp.1702–3

Kensington Palace, *A King's Feast: The Goldsmith's Art and Royal Banqueting in the 18th Century*, London, 1991

Lewis, E. (ed.), *Custom and Ceramics: Essays Presented to Kenneth Barton*, Wickham, 1991

Liefkes, R. (ed.), *Glass*, London, 1996

McKearin, H., 'Possets, Syllabubs and their Vessels', *The Glass Circle*, no.5, 1986, pp.57–67

Massingberd, H.M., and Watkin, D., *The London Ritz: A Social and Architectural History*, London, 1980

Musée National des Châteaux de Versailles et de Trianon, *Versailles et les Tables Royales en Europe, XVIIème–XIXème siècles*, Paris, 1994

Museum of London, *London Eats Out*, London, 1999

Paston-Williams, S., *The Art of Dining: A History of Cooking and Eating*, London, 1993

Pietsch, U., *Schwanenservice: Meissener Porzellan für Heinrich Graf von Brühl*, Berlin, 2000

Reinders, P., *Licks, Sticks and Bricks: A World History of Ice Cream*, Rotterdam, 1999

Savill, R., *The Wallace Collection: Catalogue of Sèvres Porcelain*, London, 1988

Schwartz, S., 'A Feast for the Eyes: 18th-Century Documents for the Creation of a Dessert Table', *International Ceramic Fair and Seminar Handbook*, London, 2000, pp.28–35

Segal, S., *A Prosperous Past: The Sumptuous Still Life in the Netherlands*, The Hague, 1988

Snodin, M., and Stavenow-Hidemark, E. (eds), *Carl and Karin Larsson: Creators of the Swedish Style*, London, 1997

Spang, R., *The Invention of the Restaurant: Paris and Modern Gastronomic Culture*, London, 2000

Stead, J., *Food and Cooking in 18th-Century Britain*, London, 1985

Thornton, P., *Seventeenth-Century Interior Decoration in England, France and Holland*, London, 1978

Truman, C., *The Sèvres Egyptian Service, 1810–12*, London, 1982

Udall, T., 'Glasses for the Dessert II: 18th-Century English Jelly and Syllabub Glasses', *The Glass Circle*, no.5, 1986, pp.33–56

Victoria and Albert Museum, *Masterpieces of Cutlery and the Art of Eating*, London, 1979

Visser, M., *The Rituals of Dinner: The Origins, Evolution, Eccentricities, and Meaning of Table Manners*, Toronto, 1991

Wheaton, B.K., *Savouring the Past: The French Kitchen and Table from 1300 to 1789*, London, 1983

Wilson, C.A., *Luncheon, Nuncheon and other Meals: Eating with the Victorians*, Leeds, 1994

Yorke, J., and Delaforce, A., *Portugal's Silver Service: A Victory Gift to the Duke of Wellington*, London, 1992

The journal *Petits Propos Culinaires* discusses both the preparation and presentation of food across the world and is available from Prospect Books, London.

INDEX

Numbers in *italic* indicate both illustrations and references in illustration captions. Further information about illustrations will be found in the Notes on the Illustrations on pages 136–41.